SCHILLER

BICENTENARY

LECTURES

London. University.

University of London
Institute of Germanic Languages
and Literatures

SCHILLER

Bicentenary Lectures

Edited by

F. Norman

Hon. Director

London
1960

Distributed by
International University Booksellers Limited
39 Store Street, London, W. C. 1

Price 21/-

PRINTED BY W S MANEY AND SON LTD LEEDS ENGLAND

CONTENTS

page

INTRODUCTORY NOTE
By F. Norman vii

SCHILLER
By Edna Purdie 1

SCHILLER AND THE COMPOSITION OF GOETHE'S *Faust*
By E. L. Stahl 24

REFLECTIONS AFTER TRANSLATING SCHILLER'S *Letters on the Aesthetic Education of Man*
By Elizabeth M. Wilkinson 46

SCHILLER AS PHILOSOPHER OF HISTORY AND AS HISTORIAN
By Benno von Wiese 83

THE STRUCTURE OF THE PERSONALITY IN SCHILLER'S TRAGEDIES
By Ilse Appelbaum-Graham 104

REFLECTIONS ON A BICENTENARY
By W. Witte 145

INTRODUCTORY NOTE

WHEN in 1949 the Conference of Teachers of German in the Universities and University Colleges of Great Britain and Ireland celebrated at their Annual Meeting, under the joint chairmanship of Professor L. A. Willoughby and the late Professor E. M. Butler, the bicentenary of the birth of Goethe a number of foreign scholars was invited to what was normally a purely domestic meeting.

At that time plans were well afoot for the foundation in the University of London of an Institute devoted to postgraduate studies in Germanic Languages and Literatures. This Institute duly began its activities in the following year under its first Director, Professor Willoughby. Much progress has been made since the Institute started its career modestly in 1950, and now that we have been celebrating the bicentenary of the birth of Schiller the Institute is happy to play its proper part by publishing the addresses that were delivered on that occasion.

As in 1949, the Conference, with the active co-operation of the English Goethe Society, invited a number of foreign scholars to its Annual Meeting. This was held from 13 to 17 July, 1959, under the chairmanship of Professor Edna Purdie, at Bedford College, London, and four of the addresses here published were delivered at that Meeting.

Professor Purdie was precluded by her exacting duties from reading a paper at the Conference, and the lecture printed here, with which the volume opens, was delivered at the German Cultural Institute in London on 13 November, 1959. It was thus intended for a wider audience and inevitably its scope and treatment differ from those of a paper addressed exclusively to academic colleagues. We are grateful to have her permission to print this lecture as a general introduction to the more specific themes that follow. Our volume would not be complete without this welcome contribution from a former Director of the Institute.

The last paper, by the Professor of German in the University of Aberdeen, W. Witte, was not delivered at the Conference either. However, Professor Witte, well-known as a Schiller scholar, took an important part in the exchange of views which followed the lectures. The ideas which he developed during these discussions were clearly so apposite and so much worth elaborating that the Secretary of the English Goethe Society, Dr. Elizabeth M. Wilkinson, promptly asked him to lecture before the Society. He did so in the library of the Institute on 29 October, 1959, and his lecture is here reprinted by kind permission of the author and of the editor of *The Publications of the English Goethe Society* from Volume XXVIII (1958/59).

Professor Stahl's address appeared in *The Germanic Review* XXXIV (1959) and is reprinted by kind permission of its general editor, Professor W. T. H. Jackson. A German version of Dr. Wilkinson's paper appeared in *Akzente* 5/1959, and a German version of Dr. Ilse Appelbaum-Graham's paper is to appear in *Jahrbuch der Deutschen Schillergesellschaft*.

Thanks are due to Dr. Christopher Middleton for his translation of the address by Professor Benno von Wiese, and to the staff of the Institute for seeing this volume through the press.

During this Conference, though not as part of it, the Institute of Germanic Languages and Literatures exhibited many of its Schiller treasures. The Institute possesses a representative collection of first and early editions of Schiller's works and it is rich in English editions and translations and in works on the poet by English scholars.

The association between the Institute and the English Goethe Society is an old established one. When the Institute was founded there was a kind of *Personalunion* between the two institutions since Professor Willoughby was simultaneously Director of the Institute and Hon. Secretary, later President, of the English Goethe Society. It was indeed due to his efforts that the valuable library of the Society was deposited at the Institute on permanent loan. This close link is further emphasized by the fact that the Meetings of the Society regularly take place in the rooms of the Institute. It is in the same tradition that the Institute is now collaborating with the Society in what is hoped will prove to be an exhaustive Bibliography of Schiller in England. It was decided to allow the bicentenary year to pass so that the material appearing in 1959 and early in 1960 could be listed. The work itself is being done by the staff of the Institute and the English Goethe Society will publish the Bibliography in its series in the autumn of 1960. In the meanwhile this volume of essays is offered by the Institute of Germanic Languages and Literatures of the University of London on behalf of English scholarship as a tribute to Schiller.

9 May, 1960 F. NORMAN

SCHILLER

By Edna Purdie

WHEN I suggested the title *Schiller* for this lecture, nothing was further from my mind than the idea that I could present a complete and rounded view of the great poet whose bicentenary is being so widely celebrated this year. Enough has been said and written about Schiller through many years and from innumerable points of view, to preclude any such misconception. What I did mean the title to imply was that I should not be attempting to approach Schiller with specialised knowledge of a particular aspect—or aspects—of his life and work; but should rather be seeking to express the substance of my own view of him after long acquaintance. For it seems to me appropriate that in this bicentenary year we should try to estimate what really constitutes our notions of Schiller—what remains in our minds as the vivid features of his art, the essentials of his outlook on the world.

And so I thought that I might try this evening to indicate what his work, so far as I have known and studied it, suggests to me about himself, and about human life, which was the subject of his deepest thought and feeling; and to point to one or two of the features of that work which have made the most lasting impression on my mind.

In the century and a half which has elapsed since Schiller's death, an immense bulk of writing has been concerned with him and with his work. He has been judged, explained, depicted from many differing standpoints; his dramas have been performed and criticised, his essays on drama, art and human living have been analysed and assessed, his portrait has been sketched, by innumerable writers. It is no easy matter to look at Schiller with an unbiased mind; it is still more difficult, perhaps, to look at him with fresh insight, or new spectacles—though a number of the books and papers appearing in 1959 have given convincing evidence that it can be done. And this is borne out by the fact that at a recent conference[1] there were wide-ranging discussions on varied aspects of his writings, which revealed both vivid interest and new points of view.

Schiller's life was not by our standards a very long one. In contrast to Goethe's, which extended from ten years before Schiller's birth to twenty-seven years beyond his death, it was almost confined to the latter half of the 18th century. His thought was unaffected by the profound changes associated with the Napoleonic wars, the development of scientific and historical methods, the influences from Europe and the East which gave new forms and impulses to poetry, drama and fiction in the earlier part of the 19th century. His life, from 1759 to 1805, spans with some measure of exactitude the great period of 18th-century thought which finds expression in the philosophy of Kant. His maturity coincided with the major European upheaval of that period—the French Revolution; indeed his first drama, *Die Räuber*, earned him the award of honorary French citizenship some eleven years after its appearance. He was attuned, in a special degree, to the feeling and temper of his age. He himself acknowledged the affinity: "Ich möchte nicht gern in einem andern Jahrhundert leben und für ein andres gearbeitet haben", he wrote in the second of the *Letters on the Aesthetic Education of Man*.

Yet few things are more noticeable about Schiller than

1 Held in London in July, 1959. See Introductory Note.

the way in which he appears in differing guise to differing epochs. To examine the history of Schiller criticism is to become aware of the chameleon. Carlyle, at the beginning of that *Life of Friedrich Schiller* which is still worth reading for the light it casts on two eminent personalities—the author and his subject—stated that Schiller's writings "are remarkable for their extent and variety as well as their intrinsic excellence; and his own countrymen are not his only, or perhaps his principal admirers". He belonged, Carlyle continues, to "that select number . . . who, having instructed their own contemporaries, are claimed as instructors by the great family of mankind, and set apart for many centuries from the common oblivion which soon overtakes the mass of authors, as it does the mass of other men". In 1905, on the centenary of Schiller's death, J. G. Robertson could write: " . . . more widely diverging views are held about Schiller to-day than about any other poet of the eighteenth century".[1] In 1949, a new English study of Schiller contained the conclusion: "If in recent years Schiller has gone a little out of fashion, the loss is ours; for it can safely be said that he is not in the least likely to go out of date".[2]

"Die Geschichte seiner Verehrung und seiner Ablehnung im 19. und frühen 20. Jahrhundert zu schreiben, wird zur dringlichen Aufgabe", writes Dr. Gerhard Storz in *Der Dichter Friedrich Schiller*, and he asserts that Thomas Mann's memorial lecture of 1955, with its depth of understanding and warmth of appreciation, marked a turning point in the attitude to Schiller in Germany in our own day.[3] Professor Benno von Wiese, in his latest

1 *Schiller after a Century.* Edinburgh & London, 1905, pp. 3-4.

2 William Witte: *Schiller.* Oxford, 1949, p. 201.

3 Gerhard Storz; *Der Dichter Friedrich Schiller,* Stuttgart, 1959, pp. 5, 8.

book on Schiller, alludes to the special difficulty presented by "der bis heute unausrottbar gebliebenen Verkennung und Verfälschung, die Schiller durch die Nachwelt gefunden hat"—adding that this is due to the praise of his admirers even more than to the criticism of his opponents.[1]

We may perhaps recall what Goethe said of Schiller to Eckermann in 1825: "Alle acht Tage war er ein anderer und [Goethe adds] ein vollendeterer."[2]

The fluctuations of Schiller's fame, inside and outside Germany, are matched by shifts of focus. The various aspects of his work command interest at different times in differing degrees. The idea of freedom has been pursued through all his dramas; all his heroes and heroines have been considered to be illustrative of different kinds and degrees of freedom. The notion of Necessity—the key to tragic hypothesis—has been similarly pursued, through the same range of central characters.[3] The close link between what Schiller thought about drama and what he presented in the dramatic form has been reexamined in England in our own day.[4] The connection between his theory of art and the speculative thought of Kant has been explored time and again; his ardent belief in the possibility of the education of human beings through knowledge has been made clear.[5] His dramas, poems and essays have a different appeal in youth, maturity, and age. None I think can deny that, in one way

1 B. von Wiese: *Friedrich Schiller*, Stuttgart, 1959, p. v.

2 *Gespräche mit Eckerman*, Gedenkausgabe, ed. E. Beutler, xxiv, p. 144 (Artemisverlag), Zürich, 1948.

3 For a balanced estimate of both *v.* Robert Petsch: *Freiheit und Notwendigkeit in Schillers Dramen*, Munich, 1905.

4 E. L. Stahl: *Friedrich Schiller's Drama. Theory and Practice*, Oxford, 1954.

5 *v.* L. A. Willoughby: "Schiller on Man's Education to Freedom through Knowledge", in *Germanic Review*, October, 1954. And we are looking forward at the moment to a new translation, by Professor Willoughby and Dr. E. M. Wilkinson, of the *Briefe über die ästhetische Erziehung des Menschen.*

or another, Schiller, after the lapse of two hundred years, has remained alive.

What is it—in our view—that accounts for this undoubted fact? That is a question on which it seems to me we might well reflect.

Schiller's life as a poet shews a tripartite form. At the outset, a tremendous outburst of dramatic energy: *Die Räuber*, *Fiesco*, *Kabale und Liebe*—three plays in three years, between 1781 and 1784, on very differing subjects, with differing *milieux* and range of characters—followed, after a retardation, by a fourth, *Don Carlos*, which emerged in 1787 as a verse tragedy, on a historical subject, with wide historical implications. At the age of 28, Schiller was an acknowledged dramatic writer. Then a middle period—a broad decade of assimilation, reflection, speculation and deduction—during which two substantial historical works were succeeded, as soon as circumstances turned favourable, by the series of essays on aesthetic subjects which occupied him from 1792 to 1796. All the well-known essays date from this period—*Über den Grund des Vergnügens an tragischen Gegenständen* and *Über die tragische Kunst; Über Anmut und Würde*, *Über das Pathetische*, and *Über das Erhabene;* the *Briefe über die ästhetische Erziehung des Menschen;* and *Über naive und sentimentalische Dichtung*. The problems of art and its rôle in human life thus constituted the fabric of his thinking in these years; to their elucidation he applied the whole of his mind and energies. There succeeded a third phase, a period of astonishing creative energy, preluded by a series of ballads which heralded his return to tragic drama; six years, in which five dramas were completed (one of which itself comprises three Parts), and a sixth was so far advanced that it remains an impressive and unfinishable fragment. The sequence of plays from *Wallenstein* through *Maria Stuart*, *Die Jungfrau von Orleans*, *Die Braut von Messina* and *Wilhelm Tell* to *Demetrius* is from any point of view a remarkable achievement. Schiller's life might well be surveyed in the image by which the youthful Goethe characterised the genius of Mahomet: the mountain cataract, gathering force as it impetuously descends, then slowly accumulating volume from tributary streams and forming a broad river in a fertile plain, flowing towards, and ultimately becoming absorbed in, the all-embracing ocean. Or we might think of his dramatic genius in different terms—might picture a well-spring, ever seeking and finding new outlets for its force; making ways for itself, now running in a subterranean channel, now emerging above ground as a potent stream. Schiller the dramatist was always experimenting in new forms and methods; however much we may trace similarities of thought and feeling in his plays, there is no one of them which does not shew him treating the new subject in a new mode. *Die Räuber* was a passionate drama of strikingly symmetrical structure; *Fiesko*, on a wider canvas, displayed a new flexibility of form; *Kabale und Liebe*, the most narrowly confined of all his dramas, shewed new vividness of character-drawing and a new pattern of opposing forces; *Don Carlos* marked a revolution in form and an immense expansion in characters and setting. Then, after the long pause, came *Wallenstein*, with its massive structure, its wide sweep of historical implications, its immense variety of personages and relationships—all dominated by the central figure, involved in the process of self-destruction. From this vast scene and impressive array of characters, Schiller turned to the narrow walls of the castle of Fotheringhay, where Maria Stuart is confined and already condemned; for the process of self-destruction he substituted one of self-conquest and self-vindication; after the broad sweep of *Wallenstein* we find in *Maria Stuart* the most delicate expression of self-knowledge, and subtle use of that process of gradual disclosure which later came to be known as "analytic technique". *Die Jungfrau von Orleans* marks a return to a large historical situation—but concentrated on an intensely personal issue. The new concept of the Maid finds expression in lyrical passages which serve to emphasise this personal aspect; and her triumphant end on the battle-field, with its bold defiance of attested fact, marks in a new way the dominance of the personal, spiritual, conflict over the historical one. Then came another change. Whereas the lyrical note in Johanna's monologues was an occasional element in the *Jungfrau*, the lyric choruses of *Die Braut von Messina* are an integral part of that play. There was here a deliberate adoption of a new mode, for reasons which Schiller set out clearly in the preface on the use of the chorus in tragedy. The lyrical passages—and Schiller wrote no lyrics that are more haunting and impressive than some of these—express reflection and judgment, applied to the sombre events and the passionate responses of human individuals to those events. They constitute a pause in the action, while at the same time they underline the significance of the forces that are at work. In form and language the *Braut* is unique in Schiller's poetic achievement; the pattern of human relations and human destiny is presented in the actual form of the drama. From the strict symmetry of this pattern Schiller passed to the looser and more pictorial mode of *Wilhelm Tell*; perhaps no greater contrast is to be found in his later works than this. The combination of typical, representative characters and vividly conveyed local scenes distinguishes the play from any other; and the non-tragic turn that is given to Tell's blow for freedom is unique. Of *Demetrius* it is not possible to speak with certainty, since it remained incomplete. But the great Reichstag scene is unrivalled, even in *Wallenstein*, for its combination of majestic sweep and realistic detail, and the foreshadowing of Marfa's dilemma shews a psychological insight only comparable with some touches in *Maria Stuart*. Schiller would seem indeed to have borne out his own conviction that every subject exacted its own appropriate form. "Jeder Stoff will seine eigene Form", he wrote to his intimate friend, Christian Gottfried Körner, on 28 July, 1800, "und die Kunst besteht darin, die ihm anpassende zu finden".

But that his mind could be fully absorbed in his own dramatic mode is evident if one looks at the translation of *Macbeth*, which he adapted for performance at Weimar in that same year 1800. The accents of the witches (previously caught with some degree of fidelity by Herder and Bürger) are here transformed into a sonorous chorus which differs in content from the original, and as far as form is concerned might have occurred in *Die Braut von Messina*:

> Aber die Meisterin wird uns schelten,
> Wenn wir mit trüglichem Schicksalswort
> Ins Verderben führen den edlen Helden,
> Ihn verlocken zu Sünd' und Mord.

And again:

> Wir streuen in die Brust die böse Saat;
> Aber dem Menschen gehört die Tat.

But equally, when he had been completely dominated by one mode, he passed with astonishing completeness and rapidity of transition to the next—his mind was at once open to the new subject, attuned to new demands. The correspondence with Körner reveals this habit of mind most clearly; extending from 1784 to Schiller's death, it is a close record of his intellectual and artistic preoccupations. And it is this richness and variety of theme and mode which constitute, to my mind, one of the lasting impressions of his art.

But if Schiller was thus remarkable in the swiftness of absorption in fresh experiments, this did not necessarily mean ease of composition. The references to

Wallenstein in the letters to Körner and Goethe are enough to refute any such assumption. The picture of Schiller's struggle with the material, drawn by Thomas Mann in the brief sketch entitled *Schwere Stunde*, convinces by its intuitive recognition of the crucial moment of artistic selection—the decision to depict the Army, the conception of *Wallensteins Lager* as the key to the tragedy; it also conveys the desperate nature of the effort involved in the final achievement of the structure.

This word structure indeed is a key-word in any analysis of Schiller's plays. He was a craftsman of extreme skill and almost unerring constructive power. It is possible to say of *Fiesco* that there are moments of uncertainty or obscurity—though careful analysis of the symbols and images of power used throughout this play reveals an underlying coherence—and arguments have always been heard on the relative importance of the two streams of action in *Wilhelm Tell*. But the double action in *Die Räuber*, the technique of representative figures in *Wallensteins Lager* and *Die Piccolomini*, the development and powerful crisis of the opposition between Maria and Elisabeth in *Maria Stuart*, the rise and fall of emotion in the *Jungfrau*, the austere sequence of disastrous moments in the *Braut*—these proofs of excellence in dramatic structure are the mark of a master playwright.

This mastery of the dramatic art is also revealed in the great scenes which remain in our memory from Schiller's plays. They are of three kinds: monologues, revealing the hidden conflicts of the spirit; duologues, where two characters present dramatic conflict in human relationships; and crowded scenes in which the cross-currents of a dramatic situation are vividly presented against a significant background. Monologues occur in almost all of Schiller's plays, but their importance varies greatly. Karl Moor, Fiesco, Ferdinand and Luise, Marquis Posa express their individual response to changing circumstances in this way. But it is in *Wallenstein* that a monologue first constitutes a great scene. For not only is an otherwise hidden inner conflict here revealed. The monologue shews us also the axis on which Wallenstein's fate revolves; the moment of apparent choice appears compellingly as the moment of destiny.

> "Wär's möglich? Könnt' ich nicht mehr, wie ich wollte?
> Nicht mehr zurück, wie mir's beliebt? Ich müsste
> Die Tat v o l l b r i n g e n , weil ich sie g e d a c h t ,
> Nicht die Versuchung von mir wies—das Herz
> Genährt mit diesem Traum, auf ungewisse
> Erfüllung hin die Mittel mir gespart,
> Die Wege bloss mir offen hab' gehalten?—
> . . . .
> Wohin denn seh' ich plötzlich mich geführt?
> Bahnlos liegt's hinter mir, und eine Mauer
> Aus meinen eignen Werken baut sich auf,
> Die mir die Umkehr türmend hemmt!

And then:–

> So hab' ich
> Mit eignem Netz verderblich mich umstrickt,
> Und nur Gewalttat kann es reissend lösen.

This great monologue—in the fourth scene of the first act of *Wallensteins Tod*—marks the decisive turn in Wallenstein's destiny; its final lines, when he has bidden his servants admit the Swedish emissary, are a weighty comment on human experience:

> Noch ist sie rein—noch! Das Verbrechen kam
> Nicht über diese Schwelle noch—So schmal ist
> Die Grenze, die zwei Lebenspfade scheidet!

The scene has greatness because with gravity and force it sets the relation of character and fate. No other monologue in the completed dramas bears this stamp so clearly; but one sketch of the later action of *Demetrius* hints at something similar in the brief indication after Demetrius has killed the murderer of the true heir to the

Russian throne—the only witness to his own hitherto unwitting usurpation: "Monolog des Demetrius. Innerer Kampf, aber überwiegendes Gefühl der Notwendigkeit, sich als Zar zu behaupten".[1] Here too there was to be the revelation of inner conflict, the record of fateful decision.

The monologues of the Maid of Orleans stand out equally from the crowded and eventful scenes of this play, but they do not to the same degree focus our attention on the process of destiny. Johanna's fateful decision is taken in a moment, in a brief scene in the press of battle; her two long monologues record, in the first place her conviction of her mission, and secondly her sense of the betrayal of that mission. They are above all expressions of personal feeling. The first combines elegiac notes of farewell to the life she has hitherto known with vigorous acceptance of the divine message; the second records with striking variations of metre and cadence the mingled feelings of passion and penitence which fill her mind and undermine her confidence, when —by yielding to a sudden human feeling of attraction— she has transgressed the conditions laid down for the fulfilment of her superhuman task. At first sight it might appear that Tell's monologue in the fourth act, while he is waiting to kill Gessler, could be compared with Wallenstein's. But there is nothing in this long justification of the deed he is about to do which transcends the sphere of rational argument, nothing which convinces us of the march of destiny. For such an effect we should rather turn to the accompanied monologues of Isabella and Don Cesar in the last scenes of the *Braut von Messina*, to that interplay of monologue and chorus which conveys, symbolically as well as through utterance, the intertwining of the individual and the whole.

Memorable scenes of dramatic conflict are equally

1 *Schillers Werke*, ed. L. Bellermann, (Bibliographisches Institut) v, p. 499, Leipzig and Vienna.

characteristic features of Schiller's plays. Foremost among them perhaps are the interview between Posa and King Philip II in *Don Carlos*, and the quarrel of the queens in *Maria Stuart*. But these two scenes have a very different importance in the action. That between Posa and Philipp serves to throw into relief the lofty (and impracticable) ideals of human living which inspire Posa's political aims—and it is noteworthy that the scene vivifies the portrait of the King, who so unexpectedly listens to the argument, more than it does that of the idealist who produces it. That between Maria and Elisabeth, invented by Schiller for his purpose, has the authentic ring of a challenge to destiny. No prisoner so apt at expressing her personality by means of defiance could expect to survive; no two persons, meeting in such mood and circumstance, could continue to co-exist. Their qualities and defects alike compel mortal combat; the quarrel is but the expression of vital incompatibility. It is surely this, even more than the magnificent, mounting invective of the speeches, that gives to the scene its quality of greatness.

The third kind of great scene that remains in the memory is that in which a crowded company of persons presents the essentials of a situation. For this particular variety of scene Schiller shewed from the outset a remarkable aptitude; the robber band in *Die Räuber* affords a notable example of a kind of collective exposition—each speaker clearly revealing individual traits of character and outlook, but being effective mainly by his association with the rest. The conspirators in *Fiesco* are also to some extent effective as a group, though their bond of association is less spectacular. But it is in *Wallensteins Lager* that we first find an unforgettable crowd scene. The delineation of the composite army, disparate and yet united, stands alone in many respects. Schiller has here accomplished the feat of individualising representative figures, so that through them we are made aware of the regional and regimental cross-currents in a mass held together by one thing alone—their faith in a successful leader. Against this mass is set the significant figure of the monk, who embodies the forces opposed to Wallenstein and in his discourse exploits every potential weakness in the mass of the army. Schiller could say in the Prologue:

> Sein Lager nur erkläret sein Verbrechen;

I think we can say that the skill with which this *Lager* is presented matches the grandeur of *Wallensteins Tod.*

Two memorable scenes in other dramas may be called "collective". The scene on the Rütli in the second act of *Wilhelm Tell* is the most powerful single scene in that drama; and I think its power derives from the vivid presentation of a united will. Here too, each single character becomes effective through association; like the members of the robber band, each one makes an individual contribution to the whole—but this "whole" is a very different one. In the Swiss confederation, resistance to the tyranny of power is a means towards a positive end: the establishment of a free and ordered community. And the scene in which the solemn oath is taken that binds the representatives of each canton to this end derives its grandeur from the concept of a united will, to which each individual harnesses his passionate revolt against injustice. The Reichstag scene in Poland at the beginning of *Demetrius* presents a wholly different situation. Here is a tribunal, before which Demetrius makes good his claim to be the true heir to the Imperial throne of Russia. There are gaps in the responses of the Senators; but the speeches of Demetrius, the Archbishop, and the Polish noble who disputes the claim and opposes war with the present Czar were completed, and the general picture of the scene is clear.

The cross-currents of the dramatic situation are discernible, against the elaborate background of the Polish assembly whose members respond in varying degree to the appeal to their emotions. The setting of this scene is as effective in its own way as was that of the Rütli; there the majesty of nature supporting the simple faith of upright men—here the traditional splendour of a proud assembly of the nation, veiling but slightly the existence of plot and counterplot.

Memorable scenes of the kind I have cited are dramatically effective, whether read in the study or seen and heard upon the stage. Their quality of greatness makes a lasting impression, so that when we think of Schiller as a dramatist they naturally come to mind. But we are bound to remember also much else that lives on in Schiller's work. He was a poet—as Goethe recognised—in whom the gift of vivid observation was combined with a native capacity for abstract thought. "Diese sonderbare Mischung von Anschauen und Abstraktion, die in Ihrer Natur ist", Goethe wrote to him on 6 October, 1795.

It was this tendency to abstraction which dominated the middle period of his life; but it is clearly enough present throughout his whole life. His mind was preoccupied with problems; a dramatic situation was seen by him as a problem expressed in human relationships. Many have discerned the idea of freedom as the central abstraction in Schiller's works. Certainly his dramatic characters are frequently shewn as striving for some kind of freedom, and sometimes attaining a different kind. Yet I think that one might formulate the central problem in Schiller's view of life in other terms. He was constantly preoccupied with the nature of man, and, consequently, with the true form of human living. From his first play to his last, the word 'Menschlichkeit' and the more abstract, universal word 'Menschheit' occur and recur.

Karl Moor in *Die Räuber*, in his frenzied rage on receiving the letter disinheriting and repudiating him, lashes out at all mankind, and dissociates himself from humanity: "Menschen haben Menschheit vor mir verborgen, da ich an Menschheit appellierte; weg dann von mir Sympathie und menschliche Schonung!", he cries in the first act. Deprived of all he holds dear in human relations, he rejects the whole concept of humanity and with it, humane feeling. Only however to recognise later the impossibility of such an attitude, and to revert to humane feeling in his final resolve to give himself up in a way which will help a poverty-stricken individual person. "Dem Mann kann geholfen werden" are the last words of the play.

Verrina's condemnation of Fiesco's assumption of power, at the end of Schiller's second play, rests on the simple relation of one human being to another: "Nicht Untertan gegen Herrn—nicht Freund gegen Freund—M e n s c h g e g e n M e n s c h red' ich zu dir". So too Ferdinand in *Kabale und Liebe* defends his love for a girl beneath his own station on the ground of pure human feeling: "Mein Entschluss und das Vorurteil! Wir wollen sehen, ob die M o d e oder die M e n s c h h e i t auf dem Platze bleiben wird." (II, 3)

The words 'Mensch', 'Menschlichkeit', 'Menschheit', recur like a refrain through *Don Carlos*. One might be tempted to see in this (as in some other features of the play) the trace of Lessing's *Nathan der Weise*, were it not for the various uses of the terms we have already observed in Schiller's earlier dramas. But it is perhaps worth noting that Lessing went on from *Nathan* to the treatise he entitled *Die Erziehung des Menschengeschlechts*, and that midway in the pause between *Don Carlos* and *Wallenstein*, Schiller wrote the *Briefe über die ästhetische Erziehung des Menschen*.

The different characters in *Don Carlos* who use these

words denoting humanity emphasise different aspects of their general significance. For Posa, the exponent of a universal brotherhood, the term 'Menschheit' signifies an abstract whole, the idea of which inspires his political aims. He claims to be its emissary in his first conversation with Carlos, when he appeals for help in the liberation of the Netherlands: he is "Ein Abgeordneter der ganzen Menschheit". This is a characteristic universalisation, as is his statement to King Philip that he cannot serve Princes because he loves humanity:

> Ich liebe
> Die Menschheit, und in Monarchien darf
> Ich niemand lieben als mich selbst. (III, 10)

In his final sacrifice of his own life he leaves a legacy to Carlos with similar implications:

> Und sagen Sie ihm, dass
> Ich Menschenglück auf seine Seele lege (IV, 21)

King Philip on the other hand speaks not in abstract but in concrete terms of his desire to find a man of clear vision and an upright mind:

> Jetzt gib mir einen Menschen, gute Vorsicht—
> Du hast mir viel gegeben. Schenke mir
> Jetzt einen Menschen! (III, 5)

Posa, with his apparently incorruptible ideals, appears to fit his definition and the King's rare confidence is bestowed upon him for this reason—despite Posa's impracticable theories, the King offers him favour:

> Ihr selbst, Ihr sollet unter meinen Augen
> Fortfahren dürfen, Mensch zu sein.

In the end, however, King Philip uses Posa's own term to describe him—basing his refusal to believe in Posa's preference of Carlos to himself upon this characteristic tendency of his mind:

> Der Freundschaft arme Flamme
> Füllt eines Posa Herz nicht aus. Das schlug
> Der ganzen Menschheit. Seine Neigung war
> Die Welt mit allen kommenden Geschlechtern.

And brooding on retaliation, the King adds with a keen appraisal:

> Er brachte
> Der Menschheit, seinem Götzen, mich zum Opfer—
> Die Menschheit büsse mir für ihn!

For Carlos alone, both 'Menschlichkeit' and 'Menschheit' denote humane feeling. For him the heart is the test of humanity.

> Die ewige
> Beglaubigung der Menschheit sind ja Tränen;
> Sein Aug' ist trocken, ihn gebar kein Weib—(II, 2)

he says on King Philip's harsh rejoinder to his pleading. And in the final issue, when he challenges the King with Posa's death:

> Natur?
> Ich weiss von keiner. Mord ist jetzt die Losung.
> Der Menschheit Bande sind entzwei. Du selbst
> Hast sie zerrissen, Sire, in deinen Reichen.

The final denial of humanity by the King, the powerlessness of Posa to substantiate his abstract conception, the losing battle of the feeling heart in Carlos—these constitute a tragic core in this long and complex drama. Did it present Schiller with the essential problem of *humanitas?*

If so, the first form his positive answer took was in the realm of speculative thought. The *Letters on the Aesthetic Education of Man*, dating from 1793 to 1795, formulate a theoretical answer to the problem which had hitherto presented itself in tragic guise. We have bestowed upon us, he asserts in the 21st Letter, "das Vermögen zur Menschheit". And it was in man's capacity for disinterested aesthetic appreciation that Schiller saw the only way to fulfil this possibility, the only means of release from the battle of opposing forces in his nature. By virtue of the impulse to pure artistry—the "play-impulse"—he might become master of himself, and therefore of his world. The non-tragic answer to the problem of the nature of man is first clearly stated in these *Briefe;* it is formulated poetically in such poems as *Die Künstler* or *Das Ideal und das Leben.* Through art alone man can apprehend the true nature of the universe, can approach reality. The opposition of sense and spirit, the extremes of feeling and reason, can only be transcended by the establishment of a harmony derived from the awareness and appreciation of beauty. "Hier also", he writes in the last of the letters on aesthetic education, "in dem Reiche des ästhetischen Scheins, wird das Ideal der Gleichheit erfüllt, welches der Schwärmer so gern auch dem Wesen nach realisirt sehen möchte". There is perhaps an echo of this in the Prologue to *Wallensteins Lager* of 1798:

> Und jetzt, an des Jahrhunderts ernstem Ende,
> Wo selbst die Wirklichkeit zur Dichtung wird,
> Wo wir den Kampf gewaltiger Naturen
> Um ein bedeutend Ziel vor Augen sehn,
> Und um der Menschheit grosse Gegenstände,
> Um Herrschaft und um Freiheit, wird gerungen,
> Jetzt darf die Kunst auf ihrer Schattenbühne
> Auch höhern Flug versuchen . . .

But of the male characters in the Wallenstein drama itself, only Max Piccolomini (apart from Gordon, for a brief moment of remorse in *Wallensteins Tod*) is preoccupied with the humane ideal expressed in the terms 'Menschheit' and 'Menschlichkeit'. This ideal forms indeed the basis of his judgment on Wallenstein's action—that judgment which it is part of his dramatic function to embody, and which he follows out, at the sacrifice of all that he holds dear. His love for Wallenstein's daughter opens his eyes to the contrast between war and peace:

> O schöner Tag, wenn endlich der Soldat
> Ins Leben heimkehrt, in die Menschlichkeit,
> Zum frohen Zug die Fahnen sich entfalten,
> Und heimwärts schlägt der sanfte Friedensmarsch. (*P.* 1, 4)

In his bitter disillusionment, in which both his father and Wallenstein are included, only this love appears pure in the whole of human experience:

> Betrug ist überall und Heuchelschein
> Und Mord und Gift und Meineid und Verrat;
> Der einzig reine Ort ist unsre Liebe,
> Der unentweihte, in der Menschlichkeit. (*W.T.* II, 7)

But in the world of *Wallenstein* deep-seated passions carry the day; those who live by the humane spirit and the feeling heart—Max and Thekla—are swept into the battle of opposing forces and choose death as the solution. Wallenstein himself, who attains tragic grandeur in the downfall of his hopes, does not at any time shew awareness of a true humanity. The contrast between him and Maria Stuart is nowhere more acute than in this respect. For the Maria of the first and third acts, the word 'menschlich' is associated with fault or error:

> Ich habe menschlich, jugendlich gefehlt,
> Die Macht verführte mich—

she acknowledges in the angry exchanges with Elisabeth. But by the end she has attained a humanity which conquers passion and endows her with not only courage but tranquillity; for the first time in Schiller's dramas the non-tragic answer to the problem of human living is given in a tragedy.

There is an initial contrast between human and divine ('menschlich' and 'göttlich') in the *Jungfrau von Orleans;* this contrast is also transformed in the course of the drama. Johanna, always aware of humane feeling, deems herself debarred by the terms of her mission from acting in accordance with it; thus she is finally convinced of her own guilt in sparing the life of Lionel, in allowing human love to affect a superhuman mission. But by suffering silently a false charge, she—like Maria—atones for a different fault; and she too emerges triumphant from this process of expiation. It is a triumph differently expressed —in outward forms of miracle and victory; but it similarly reflects the inner clarification of desire and motive which alone renders possible the reconciliation or fusion of human and divine that is symbolised in the manner of her death.

Nowhere in Schiller's works is the problem of the relation between the human individual and superhuman powers more sharply and uncompromisingly presented than in *Die Braut von Messina*. Ambiguous oracles and violent passions plunge human beings into disastrous confusion; secrecy and coincidence play almost indistinguishable parts in the swift sequences of calamity and discovery. In the ruin of her hopes and in her vehement despair Isabella expresses a profound and bitter scepticism that recalls the feelings of another ill-fated parent:

> As flies to wanton boys, are we to the gods,—
> They kill us for their sport.[1]

It is only in Don Cesar's decision to atone by his own death for his murder of his brother that any possibility of reconciliation between gods and men is suggested; and this possibility rests upon man's own act of will:

> Der Tod hat eine reinigende Kraft,
> In seinem unvergänglichen Palaste
> Zu echter Tugend reinem Diamant
> Das Sterbliche zu läutern und die Flecken
> Der mangelhaften Menschheit zu verzehren.

The first appearance of Tell is linked with humane feeling:

> Wer ist der Mann, der hier um Hilfe fleht?

and then:

> Die Stunde dringt, dem Mann muss Hilfe werden. (I, I)

1 *King Lear*, IV, I.

The opposition between the Swiss people and their tyrannical masters is that of freedom and oppression; but it could equally well be described as the contrast between humanity and inhumanity. It is not only Tell who expresses humane feeling; Gertrud Stauffacher, the Freiherr von Attinghausen, Bertha von Bruneck, all sound a similar note. Against this we see the utter lack of humane feeling in Gessler and his underlings, and hear of it in the other Landvögte. But it is Tell who in this respect plays the representative rôle. This is evident in the final conversation between him and Johannes Parricida after the murder of the Emperor. Parricida appeals to Tell's humanity:

> O wenn Ihr Mitleid fühlt und Menschlichkeit—

and the appeal is reluctantly admitted:

> Doch stehet auf—Was Ihr auch Grässliches
> Verübt—Ihr seid ein Mensch—Ich bin es auch—
> Vom Tell soll keiner ungetröstet scheiden—
> Was ich vermag, das will ich tun. (v, 2)

Thus humane feeling, while it does not obscure moral judgment, is exalted above it. He who is truly free is humane.

An echo of this is to be heard in a speech of Demetrius in the first scene:

> Wer aber soll gerecht sein auf der Erde,
> Wenn es ein grosses, tapfres Volk nicht ist
> Das frei in höchster Machtvollkommenheit . . .
> Der schönen Menschlichkeit gehorchen kann?

Demetrius insists upon the bond of brotherhood between men:

> Ich bin erwachsen in der Niedrigkeit;
> Das schöne Band hab' ich verehren lernen,
> Das Mensch an Mensch mit Wechselneigung bindet.

And King Sigismund strikes the same chord when he

exhorts Demetrius to revere his mother:

Kein bessres Pfand für Eure Menschlichkeit
Hat Euer Volk als Eure Kindesliebe.

It would seem that in the future conflict between truth and falsehood in the heart of Marfa and in the mind of Demetrius, humane feeling was to be a powerful factor.

I think the notion of 'Menschheit' is at the heart of Schiller's work. Most of those who have written about him have used, sooner or later, the word idealism, or optimism, to characterise his ethical standpoint and his outlook upon life. And if to believe in the possibility of developing and perfecting the essential humanity of man is to be an optimist, Schiller may indeed be called one. But it is important to realise the nature of his optimism. Faith in perfectibility did not obscure his vision of the actual. Youthful idealists in his dramas die in the hey-day of their energy and powers; Karl Moor, Ferdinand, Posa, Max Piccolomini, Mortimer—none of them finds before he succumbs that balance or harmony which would complete his humanity. The characters who do reach maturity and harmony of soul are outwardly defeated by opposing forces of the world in which they live. Schiller did not disregard the sombre power of evil within the hearts of men, nor underestimate its effect upon the forms of human living. For the most part, he looked on the continuing struggle of mankind with the eyes of the tragic poet, seeing clearly the desperate nature of the conflict; only in *Wilhelm Tell* does the dramatic situation solve itself outwardly in conciliatory fashion. And it is perhaps significant that Schiller proceeded straightway to work upon a drama in which a tragic outcome is quite certainly foreshadowed. There is not to my mind any doubt that he saw the world in terms of a dramatic conflict, whose issue was uncertain. But equally I think he believed in a favourable issue; he believed that man has the capacity to become aware of good, and that by the disinterested pursuit, through effort and suffering, of what he recognises to be the good, he can develop into a wholly harmonised being, and so fulfil his own humanity and be at one with his destiny—be

Mit dem Geschick in hoher Einigkeit (*Die Künstler*).

In the recurrent crises of the history of the human race, it is surely still a vital notion here that Schiller offers. He offers it in twofold form: through what he says in his own person, and through what he sees and puts before us in the form of drama.

SCHILLER AND THE COMPOSITION OF GOETHE'S *FAUST*

By E. L. Stahl

At an early stage of their friendship, in 1794, Schiller asked Goethe for news on *Faust*. Goethe gave an evasive answer, intimating his unwillingness to broach that vast problem. Three years later, in June, 1797, Schiller was surprised and delighted to learn about his friend's resumption of work on the great fragment. On 23 June, Goethe noted in his *Tagebuch* the composition of an "ausführliches Schema" and on the following day wrote the *Zueignung*.

To what extent did Schiller contribute to the progress Goethe was able to make between 1794 and 1797? For a clear answer it would be invaluable to know how much of the text had been written down at that time. The *Fragment* is probably all that Schiller saw of the drama itself. On 17 July, 1795, Wilhelm von Humboldt acknowledged the receipt of a letter from Schiller, not preserved for us, with an account of Goethe's plan for *Faust* which Humboldt considered "ungeheuer". We also know that Goethe reported a version of the Helena-scenes to Schiller in September, 1800. There is no evidence to show that he imparted to him those scenes of *Der Tragödie Erster Teil* which are not found in the *Fragment*.

It has recently been argued by Ernst Grumach with his customary learning and skill that Goethe had in fact written more of the *Prolog im Himmel* than is generally agreed, when he returned to *Faust* in June, 1797. Grumach acknowledges some influence as far as the resumption of work is concerned, but believes that Schiller had no share in the composition of the *Prolog:* "In keinem Fall kann das, was wir als die leitende Idee des Ganzen empfinden, sich erst im Laufe der 90er Jahre unter dem Einfluss Schillers gebildet haben".[1] The argument is based largely on the evidence provided by the manuscript of the only portion of the *Prolog* in its first version that has come down to us. It is not the portion containing the line: "Es irrt der Mensch, solang' er strebt," which will always be held to express one of the leading themes of Goethe's *Faust*. This "leitende Idee," I hope to show, may well have been introduced into the drama during the early years of the friendship with Schiller and owe something to his influence.

While it is impossible to say, in view of the fact that the relevant material has been so fragmentarily preserved, whether the *Prolog* in its earliest form contained the idea of "Streben," it is remarkable that with the sole exception of line 1858, all instances of the word occurring in Part I, used as a verb as well as a noun, belong to those portions of *Faust* which were first published in 1808. It is not to be found in the *Urfaust* and only once in the *Fragment*. Although Goethe used the word significantly in *Tasso*, in this drama it does not have the importance of representing a cardinal theme which it undoubtedly has in *Faust*. On the whole the same is true of the words "Genuss" and "Tätigkeit" comprising complementary themes related to "Streben".[2] These words are also

1 E. Grumach, "Prolog und Epilog im Faustplan von 1797", *Goethe*, XIII (1951), 70.

2 In a draft letter to an unknown person, Goethe on 1 May, 1801, called "Genuss" and "Streben" "die beiden Enden menschlicher Tätigkeit". Cf. also his letter to Schiller of 25 March, 1801: "Beim Nachdenken übers Beharrende im Menschen, worauf sich die Phänomene der Kultur beziehen liessen, habe ich bis jetzt nur vier Grundzustände gefunden: des Geniessens, des Strebens, der Resignation, der Gewohnheit". The following are the most important lines in which the words occur in *Faust*, Part I: *Streben:* 317, 697, 716, 767, 912, 1075, 1099, 1353, 1676, 1742, 1858, 4116 The most striking instances are those occurring in portions of the play which Goethe composed between 1797 and 1800. *Genuss:* 774, 1696, 1756, 1766, 3250 f. *Tat*, *Tätigkeit:* 215, 340, 632, 705, 712, 1237, 1600, 1629.

used emphatically and programmatically in the all-important first Paralipomenon which Goethe wrote down some time after 1797 and dated, in a revised version, 11 April, 1800:

> Ideales Streben nach Einwirken und Einfühlen in die ganze Natur. Erscheinung des Geists als Welt und Taten Genius. Streit zwischen Form und Formlosen. Vorzug dem formlosen Gehalt vor der leeren Form. Gehalt bringt die Form mit. Form ist nie ohne Gehalt. Diese Widersprüche statt sie zu vereinigen disparater zu machen. Helles, kaltes wissenschaftliches Streben Wagner. Dumpfes warmes wissenschaftliches Streben Schüler. Lebens Genuss der Person von aussen gesehen: Erster Teil. In der Dumpfheit Leidenschaft. Taten Genuss nach aussen Zweiter und Genuss mit Bewusstsein. Schönheit. Schöpfungs Genuss von innen. Epilog im Chaos auf dem Weg zur Hölle.

The language of the Paralipomenon is of great interest. The key words are "Streben" and "Genuss"; others merit some attention, although they are less important for understanding Goethe's intentions at that time. Faust begins "in der Dumpfheit Leidenschaft". The word "Dumpfheit" occurs frequently in Goethe's early writings, particularly in the diaries between 1776 and 1780.[1] In the *Sturm und Drang* period he used it to denote a fertile irrational state of mind from which all creative activity is derived. Thus he wrote in the "rhapsody" on nature in 1780: "Sie hüllt den Menschen in Dumpfheit ein und spornt ihn ewig zum Lichte".[2] This idea is all but Faustian. Later Goethe came to regard that primordial state more and more as a condition to be overcome by conscious and deliberate striving towards clarity, without entirely giving up the notion of guidance by a higher power. In this sense he wrote in the opening stanza of

1 Cf. R. M. Meyer, "Studien zu Goethes Wortgebrauch", *Archiv für das Studium der neueren Sprachen*, XCVI, esp. pp. 3 et seq. and Ewald A. Boucke, "Wort und Bedeutung in Goethes Sprache, *Litterarhistorische Forschungen*, ed. Schick & Waldberg, Heft XX. (1901), esp. pp. 156 et seq.

2 *Werke*, Weimar edition, Abt. 2, Vol. XI. p. 7.

the poem *Abschied*, composed in 1800 and projected as a pendant to *Zueignung*:

> Wer schildert gern den Wirrwarr des Gefühles
> Wenn ihn der Weg zur Klarheit aufgeführt?

In the same way Schiller, in his classical period, considered "Dumpfheit" to be the mark of the animal state of man: "Mitten in seiner Tierheit überrascht den Menschen der Trieb zum Absoluten—und da in diesem dumpfen Zustande alle seine Bestrebungen bloss auf das Materielle und Zeitliche gehen . . . so wird er durch jene Forderung bloss veranlasst . . . anstatt nach Form, nach einem unversiegenden Stoff . . . zu streben".[1] Not merely Faust, but also the Schüler is possessed by "Dumpfheit" in his first stage, according to the Paralipomenon. He forms a contrast to Wagner, whose "Streben" is "hell" and "kalt".

Wagner and the Schüler are also opposed as "formloser Gehalt" and "leere Form", a contrast which Goethe intended to accentuate at the time when he wrote the Paralipomenon, but which he eventually toned down in the second part of *Faust*. It has often been remarked that in making this distinction between "leere Form" and "formloser Gehalt" he was beginning to treat the problem of his drama in terms of the aesthetic theories current at the time. His own *Der Sammler und die Seinen* and Schiller's letters on aesthetic education, among others, amply testify to the significance they both gave to the relationship between the essential components of every product of art and of nature.

In another context, in his *Materialien zur Geschichte der Farbenlehre*, Goethe made a distinction that closely

1 *Briefe über die ästhetische Erziehung des Menschen*, Letter 24.

resembles the one he noted in the Paralipomenon:

Gehalt ohne Methode führt zur Schwärmerei
Methode ohne Gehalt zum leeren Klügeln
Stoff ohne Form zum beschwerlichen Wissen
Form ohne Stoff zum hohlen Wähnen.

The two friends frequently discussed the *Farbenlehre* during the years 1797 and 1798, when *Faust* also figured prominently in their correspondence and their conversations.[1]

Although the terms "Dumpfheit", "Form", and "Gehalt" are used significantly in the Paralipomenon, they do not hold the same interest in a discussion of the composition of *Faust* as do the words "Streben", "Genuss", and "Tätigkeit".

A recently published fascicle of *Grimms Wörterbuch* gives, in admirable detail, an historical account of the word "Streben" and very properly assigns to Goethe pride of place. But there are surprising gaps. Gottsched and Fichte deserve to be mentioned in any history of the word. The former writes, in almost Goethean terms:

> Die Tugend ist eine Fertigkeit, seine Handlungen nach dem Gesetze der Natur einzurichten. Nun gebeut uns das Gesetz der Natur, nach der Vollkommenheit überhaupt zu streben, dieselbe auch bei andern zu befördern und in allen seinen Handlungen eine Übereinstimmung zu beobachten.[2]
>
> Da nun die Vollkommenheiten des Menschen dreierlei sind, nämlich der Seele, des Leibs, und des äusserlichen Zustandes: so sieht man wohl, dass es unsre Pflicht sei, nach allen Gattungen derselben zu streben, so viel als in unserm Vermögen steht, und keine einzige derselben geringe zu schätzen.[3]

[1] New evidence has shown how actively Schiller participated in the work. Cf. R. Matthaei, "Neue Funde zu Schillers Anteil an Goethes Farbenlehre", *Goethe*, xx. (1958), 155 et seq.

[2] *Erste Gründe der Gesamten Weltweisheit*, 10. Auflage (Leipzig, 1736), para. 50.

[3] Ibid., para. 531.

Fichte had a leading share in formulating the idea of striving as it gained currency at the end of the eighteenth century. One cannot do better than quote Wilhelm Wundt on Fichte's philosophy:

> Die Produktivität des Bewusstseins steht im Mittelpunkt seiner ganzen Gedankenbildung . . . Dieses Produktionsvermögen äussert sich als unendliches Streben . . . Das Ich ist sich seiner Tätigkeit zunächst nicht bewusst und ringt sich erst im Fortgang seines Strebens zur Klarheit empor.[1]

> In dem Begriff des Strebens ist der Begriff der Schranke unmittelbar mit enthalten. Das Ich strebt ins Unendliche, aber es vermöchte nicht zu streben, wenn sich ihm nicht beständig Schranken entgegensetzten, die es überwindet, um auf weitere Schranken zu stossen, über die es abermals hinausstrebt.[2]

Fichte's idea of "Streben" and that encountered in *Faust* are strikingly similar. One difference must be noted. For Fichte the progress towards "Klarheit" is achieved by the deliberate effort of the individual human being. In Goethe's drama it is the Lord who will *lead* Faust "in die Klarheit". The significance of this difference will become apparent later.

There can, of course, be no justification for assuming that Goethe took over Fichte's concept into his play and merely modified it to suit his dramatic purpose. But it remains noteworthy that he participated in repeated discussions on the *Wissenschaftslehre*, where the theory of "Streben" is most clearly stated, and that these discussions took place in Schiller's home at Jena three months before Goethe recommenced work on *Faust*.

1 Wilhelm Wundt, *Fichteforschungen* (Stuttgart, 1929), pp. 59 ff.

2 Wilhelm Wundt, *J. G. Fichte* (Stuttgart, 1927), p. 124. Fichte's theory of "Streben" is contained in the section of the *Grundlage der gesammten Wissenschaftslehre* entitled *Grundlage der Wissenschaft des Praktischen* (*Sämmtliche Werke* [Berlin, 1845], I. pp. 246 et. seq. esp. pp. 261-291).

He made the following entries in his *Tagebuch* for 1797:

> 12 *March:* Zu Schiller... Nach Tische Legations Rat Humboldt über Fichtes neue Darstellung der Wissenschaftslehre im philosophischen Journal.
>
> 14 *March:* Abends zu Schiller, wo Legations Rat von Humboldt war und Fichtens neue Darstellung der Wissenschaftslehre aus dem philosophischen Journal vorgelesen wurde.
>
> 16 *March:* ... dann zu Schiller, wo der Legations Rat die neue Darstellung der Wissenschaftslehre weiter vorlas.
>
> 19 *March:* Nach Tische Legations Rat von Humboldt und Niethammer; die Fichtesche Theorie ward durchgesprochen.

These meetings were not entirely to his taste, as he frankly avowed in a letter to Knebel on 28 March, 1797, informing him"dass ich bei der spekulativen Tendenz des Kreises, in dem ich lebe, wenigstens im Ganzen Anteil daran nehmen muss", but also confiding "dass man manchmal nicht wissen mag, wo einem der Kopf steht". "Ich freue mich daher", he goes on to say, "bald wieder nach Weimar zu kommen, um mich wieder in einem andern Kreise zu erholen".

His interest in Fichte's ideas is nevertheless strongly attested. The *Versuch einer neuen Darstellung der Wissenschaftslehre* is a summary of the cardinal principles of Fichte's philosophy, with only a brief statement on the importance of "Streben". This had been more amply stated in the *Grundlage der gesammten Wissenschaftslehre* of 1794. Goethe received a copy of this as well as one of the treatise *Über den Begriff der Wissenschaftslehre* in that year and read at least a portion of it with some care. He underlined passages in the section entitled *Hypothetische Einteilung der Wissenschaftslehre*, which mentions the theory of "Streben", and he also heavily marked, among others, the following sentence from an earlier part of the work: "Im menschlichen Geiste ist also ursprünglich vor unserem Wissen vorher Gehalt und Form, und beide sind unzertrennlich verbunden".[1] It is impossible to say whether he scored these passages before or after his visit to Jena in March, 1797, but their relevance for the dating of the first Paralipomenon is incontestable.

If the theory of "Streben" formed an important part of the Jena discussions, as it very probably did, Goethe and Schiller could make a positive contribution, for both of them had tellingly used the word in their earlier writings. "Damals sehnte ich mich", Werther says on 9 May, "in glücklicher Unwissenheit hinaus in die unbekannte Welt, wo ich für mein Herz so viele Nahrung, so vielen Genuss hoffte, meinen strebenden, sehnenden Busen auszufüllen und zu befriedigen". This is a characteristically Wertherian formulation. "Streben" aims at "Genuss" which is equated with "Nahrung", and "Streben" is also identified with "Sehnen" which Fichte characterizes as a vague feeling devoid of any concrete direction or objective, "Tätigkeit, die gar kein Objekt hat" or "Trieb nach etwas völlig unbekanntem, das sich bloss durch ein Bedürfnis, durch ein Missbehagen, durch eine Leere offenbart, die Ausfüllung sucht, und nicht andeutet, woher?"[2] This kind of aimless striving Goethe later came to regard as one of the marks of the dilettante opposed to the quality of the true artist: "Der wahre Künstler steht fest und sicher auf sich selbst; sein Streben, sein Ziel ist der höchste Zweck der Kunst . . . Dilettanten oder eigentliche Pfuscher scheinen im Gegenteil nicht nach einem Ziel zu streben".[3] "Streben", "Genuss", and "Tätigkeit" are differently co-ordinated in *Werther* and in *Faust*. Werther's idleness contrasts with Faust's more purposeful activity. Already part and parcel of the

1 Cf. R. Neumann, *Goethe und Fichte* (Berlin, 1904), pp. 47 et seq.

2 *Sämmtliche Werke* (Berlin, 1845), I. pp. 302 f.

3 *Über den sogenannten Dilettantismus*, in collaboration with Schiller and Meyer, 1799.

Urfaust, "Tätigkeit" assumes increasingly greater importance as Goethe continued to write the play after 1797. Here again Fichte, and Schiller, could help him to clarify his own intentions. The *Vorlesungen über die Bestimmung des Gelehrten*, first published in 1794, contain a passage that could win Goethe's approbation at the time he wrote the *Prolog im Himmel*:

> Der Mensch is von Natur faul und träge. Nicht das Bedürfnis ist die Quelle des Lasters; es ist Antrieb zur Tätigkeit und zur Tugend; die Faulheit ist die Quelle aller Laster . . . Es ist kein Heil für den Menschen, ehe nicht diese natürliche Trägheit mit Glück bekämpft ist und ehe nicht der Mensch in der Tätigkeit und allein in der Tätigkeit seine Freude und seinen Genuss findet. Dazu ist das Schmerzhafte, das mit dem Gefühl des Bedürfnisses verbunden ist. Es soll zur Tätigkeit reizen.[1]

If we substitute "unbedingte Ruh" for Fichte's "Trägheit" and the spirit of negation for his feeling of want, one of the leading ideas of the *Prolog im Himmel* may be said to agree exactly with this statement, which forms part of an attack upon Rousseau and recalls Schiller's rejection of the same philosopher's ideal of physical ease in *Über naive und sentimentalische Dichtung*.

Schiller links the ideas of activity and of striving in a passage written as early as 1786 in *Philosophische Briefe:* "Alle Geister . . . streben nach dem Zustand der höchsten freien Äusserung ihrer Kräfte, alle besitzen den gemeinschaftlichen Trieb, ihre Tätigkeit auszudehnen . . ."[2] In the *Philosophische Briefe* he also states a principle of theodicy which resembles Goethe's own, as presented in *Faust:* "Dieser erfinderische Geist", Schiller asks, referring to God, "sollte nicht auch den Irrtum zu seinen grossen Zwecken verbrauchen?" and he goes on to conclude: "Jede Fertigkeit der Vernunft,

1 *Sämmtliche Werke*, VI. p. 343.

2 *Sämtliche Werke*, Säkularausgabe, XI. p. 119.

auch im Irrtum, vermehrt ihre Fertigkeit zu Empfängnis der Wahrheit".[1]

If the agreement between Goethe and Schiller on this important issue has considerable significance, the observations which Schiller offered on the character of Wilhelm Meister in letters written during July, 1796, have an even more direct bearing on the composition of the first part of *Faust*:

> Sein Wert [Schiller writes] liegt in seinem Gemüt, nicht in seinen Wirkungen, in seinem Streben, nicht in seinem Handeln; daher muss ihm sein Leben, sobald er einem andern davon Rechenschaft geben will, so gehaltleer vorkommen.[2]

> Wenn ich das Ziel, bei welchem Wilhelm nach einer langen Reihe von Verirrungen endlich anlangt, mit dürren Worten auszusprechen hätte, so würde ich sagen: "Er tritt von einem leeren und unbestimmten Ideal in ein bestimmtes tätiges Leben, aber ohne die idealisierende Kraft dabei einzubüssen". . . . Dass er nun, unter der schönen und heitern Führung der Natur (durch Felix) von dem Idealischen zum Reellen, von einem vagen Streben zum Handeln und zur Erkenntnis des Wirklichen übergeht, ohne doch dasjenige dabei einzubüssen, was in jenem ersten strebenden Zustand Reales war, dass er Bestimmtheit erlangt, ohne die schöne Bestimmbarkeit zu verlieren, dass er sich begrenzen lernt, aber in dieser Begrenzung selbst, durch die Form, wieder den Durchgang zum Unendlichen findet usf., dieses nenne ich die Krise seines Lebens, das Ende seiner Lehrjahre . . .[3]

Much of this may be applied to Faust and indeed when Schiller came to obey Goethe's demand of 22 June, 1797, to consider the fragment "und so mir meine eignen Träume, als ein wahrer Prophet, zu erzählen und zu deuten", he stressed, on the one hand, the "symbolische

1 Ibid., p. 132.

2 5 July.

3 8 July. An echo of Schiller's remarks may be found in the words which Jarno addresses to Wilhelm in the fifth chapter of the eighth book: "Der Mensch ist nicht eher glücklich, als bis sein unbedingtes Streben sich selbst seine Begrenzung bestimmt".

Bedeutsamkeit" of the plot, and, on the other, the need "dass der Faust in das handelnde Leben geführt würde".[1]

Goethe met both demands, but in his own idiosyncratic way. He persistently refused to commit his work to a philosophical idea which Schiller as perseveringly urged upon him. It is idle to deny that he had an idea for the whole, although he was right to repudiate its abstract and its all-pervading qualities: "Und ferner, dass der Teufel die Wette verliert, und dass ein aus schweren Verirrungen immerfort zum Bessern aufstrebender Mensch zu erlösen sei, das ist zwar ein wirksamer, manches erklärender Gedanke, aber es ist keine Idee, die dem Ganzen und jeder einzelnen Szene im besondern zugrunde liege".[2] We may call this a religious theme; it is certainly not a philosophical idea in Schiller's sense.

Here we reach the limits of Schiller's influence upon *Faust* as upon other works of Goethe. In the last resort even their notions of "Streben" are not entirely the same. When we recall the line: "Es irrt der Mensch solang' er strebt" or Goethe's reference to the "düstere, unbefriedigte Streben der Hauptfigur",[3] it becomes clear that he did not only stress the positive side of what, for Schiller and Fichte, possessed innate value and mainly stood in need of being transformed into practical activity, an end that could be achieved by the exertion of human will-power. In this there is more agreement between Goethe and Hölderlin, who also took up the theme in the nineties and asserted the disruptive effect of human striving.[4] As late as 1822 Goethe said of Adele Schopen-

1 Letters of 23 and 26 June, 1797.

2 To Eckermann, 6 May, 1827.

3 To Eckermann, 3 May, 1827.

4 *Sämmtliche Werke*, ed. Hellingrath, III. p. 301. Even Schiller, however, voiced his scepticism in *Würde der Frauen* (1795):

Feindlich ist des Mannes Streben,
Mit zermalmender Gewalt
Geht der Wilde durch das Leben
Ohne Rast und Aufenthalt.

hauer's *Gabriele*, contrasting the task of the novelist with that of the educator:

> Der Roman hingegen stellt das Unbedingte als das Interessanteste vor, gerade das grenzenlose Streben, was uns aus der menschlichen Gesellschaft, was uns aus der Welt treibt: unbedingte Leidenschaft, für die dann bei unübersteiglichen Hindernissen nur Befriedigung im Verzweifeln bleibt, Ruhe nur im Tod.

This might have been Faust's fate, as it was Werther's, if Goethe had not been able to view the problem of human effort in the light of a different principle from that upheld by Schiller. The intricate question of Faust's guilt apart, long before the final solution is reached with the angels' words:

> "Wer immer strebend sich bemüht
> Den können wir erlösen"

the inadequacy of unaided "Streben" as a means to achieve salvation has been presented to us. "Streben" is never for Goethe an end in itself and at its highest it finds its true consummation with surcease beyond this world, in *Faust* no less than in *Weltseele*:

> Und bald verlischt ein unbegrenztes Streben
> Im sel'gen Wechselblick.
> Und so empfangt mit Dank das schönste Leben
> Vom All ins All zurück.

The essential difference between Goethe's and Schiller's points of view becomes manifest when we consider the latter's observations on the "Turmgesellschaft" in *Wilhelm Meisters Lehrjahre*. His attitude is curiously ambivalent. On the one hand he demands a more philosophical treatment of the principle guiding that Society, on the other he attempts to divert Goethe from using religious ideas by lauding the purely aesthetic tendencies of the work:

> Aber im Ernste—woher mag es kommen, dass Sie einen Menschen haben erziehen und fertig machen können, ohne auf Bedürfnisse zu stossen, denen die Philosophie nur begegnen

> kann? Ich bin überzeugt, dass dieses bloss der ästhetischen Richtung zuzuschreiben ist, die Sie in dem ganzen Roman genommen. Innerhalb der ästhetischen Geistesstimmung regt sich kein Bedürfnis nach jenen Trostgründen, die aus der Spekulation geschöpft werden müssen . . . Die gesunde und schöne Natur braucht, wie Sie selbst sagen, keine Moral, kein Naturrecht, keine politische Metaphysik: Sie hätten ebenso gut auch hinzusetzen können, sie braucht keine Gottheit, keine Unsterblichkeit, um sich zu stützen und zu halten.[1]

Later in the same letter Schiller says:

> Könnte ich nur in Ihre Denkweise dasjenige einkleiden, was ich im Reich der Schatten und in den Ästhetischen Briefen der meinigen gemäss ausgesprochen habe, so wollten wir sehr bald einig sein.

This remained a vain hope. The mature Schiller consistently disavowed the value of belief in immortality. His "Reich der Schatten" in *Das Ideal und das Leben* is the region "wo die reinen Formen wohnen", an Olympian realm which the demi-god Hercules could bodily enter, while

> Zwischen Sinnenglück und Seelenfrieden
> Bleibt dem Menschen nur die bange Wahl.

In an earlier poem, *Resignation* (1784), Schiller had stated this alternative even more harshly through the words of the invisible "Genius":

> Geniesse, wer nicht glauben kann! Die Lehre
> Ist ewig wie die Welt. Wer glauben kann, entbehre!
> Die Weltgeschichte ist das Weltgericht.

The two alternatives "Hoffnung und Genuss" are posed in a mutually exclusive antithesis not implied in the thematic relation between the "Streben" and the "Genuss" of Goethe's *Faust*, and the poem contains a sharp animadversion against the "Fieberwahn Unsterblichkeit".

In his earliest period, on the other hand, Schiller had accepted a rudimentary form of belief in immortality: "Die Materie zerfährt in ihre letzten Elemente wieder,

[1] Letter of 9 July, 1796.

die nun in anderen Formen und Verhältnissen durch die Reiche der Natur wandern, anderen Absichten zu dienen. Die Seele fähret fort, in anderen Kreisen ihre Denkkraft zu üben und das Universum von anderen Seiten zu beschauen".[1] This is the young Schiller's final conclusion based on the premiss: "Vollkommenheit des Menschen liegt in der Übung seiner Kräfte durch Betrachtung des Weltplans". He gave up this belief when he began to study Kant's critical philosophy and he never returned to it. But Goethe retained a similar belief throughout his life and presented it with inimitable poetic power in *Faust*.

Schiller's "classical" philosophy, the idealism which he adopted after reading Kant, is firmly founded on the view that man is endowed with powers of reason and of will whose exercise can ensure the achievement of his destiny in this life. "Die Unsterblichkeit" he wrote to Körner on 30 March, 1789, explaining the meaning of the eighteenth section of *Die Künstler*, "ist ein Produkt des Gefühls für Ebenmass, nach dem der Mensch die moralische Welt beurteilen wollte, ehe er diese genug überschaute". He expressed a similar sentiment in the epigram *Unsterblichkeit:*

> Vor dem Tod erschrickst du! Du wünschest, unsterblich zu leben?
> Leb' im Ganzen! Wenn du lange dahin bist, es bleibt.

Goethe found it impossible to solve the problem of Wilhelm Meister's "Bildung" without affirming the principle of educative guidance. Much less could he find a solution for Faust's "Streben" without the postulation of divine guardianship involving the notion of immortality. The *Prolog im Himmel* probably owed something to Schiller where the presentation of the problem of "Streben" is concerned. In its transcendental solution

1 *Über den Zusammenhang der tierischen Natur des Menschen mit seiner geistigen* (1780) (*Sämmtliche Werke*, Säkularausgabe, XI. p. 79).

he had no share. Above all, Goethe was in no way indebted to him for the original conception of the dramatic issue which Ernst Grumach's profound and far-reaching investigations have set in a new light: 'Faust sollte ein Spiel werden von der neuen Versuchung Adams, von dem letzten vernichtenden Anschlag Lucifers gegen den Menschen, der durch Christus gerettet wird'.[1] Nor does Schiller appear to have exerted any direct influence upon Goethe, although he may have done so indirectly, when this grandiose design was changed some time after 1797 to give us the present, no less exalted and sublime ending.

In Goethe's view plants, like men, experience a process of "Bildung": they may even display an elementary form of "Streben", as the poem *Metamorphose der Pflanzen* shows, and for these morphological processes he was prepared to accept the postulation of divine activity, the view "dass wir, um das Vorhandene zu betrachten, eine vorhergegangene Tätigkeit zugeben müssen und dass, wenn wir uns eine Tätigkeit denken wollen, wir derselben ein schicklich Element unterlegen, worauf sie wirken konnte, und dass wir zuletzt diese Tätigkeit mit dieser Unterlage als immerfort zusammen bestehend und ewig gleichzeitig vorhanden denken müssen. Dieses Ungeheure, personifiziert, tritt uns als ein Gott entgegen, als Schöpfer und Erhalter, welchen anzubeten, zu verehren und zu preisen wir auf alle Weise aufgefordert werden".[2] Fichte, like Schelling, appears to have had a profounder intuition of this side of Goethe's work. A hitherto unknown passage on *Faust* from the ill-starred essay *Über Geist und Buchstab in der Philosophie* of 1795 has recently come to light:

> Im ganzen Künstlerlaufe des Dichters scheint dieses Stück mir nicht so zersplittert und Fragment, als einige glauben. Ich

1 Loc. cit. p. 107.

2 *Bildungstrieb* (*Zur Morphologie*, 1820). The essay ends with a "Schema" in which "Stoff" and "Form" flank "Vermögen", "Kraft", "Gewalt", "Streben", and "Trieb" and together produce "Leben".

> sehe im Geist Faust nach seinem misslungenen Herumtreiben nach aussen, in sich einkehren, da den Frieden finden, den er ausser sich vergeblich suchte, und durch die Prüfung geläutert nach den Gesetzen einer wundervollen und doch natürlichen Metempsychose ihn in der Iphigenie wieder hervorgehen.[1]

Fichte may not have meant to say more than that Goethe was bound to make Faust settle down eventually to a calmer life, comparable with that of Iphigenie after her return to Greece—he could not know that Goethe planned to write a sequel with a very different intention—and his reason for omitting the passage in the published version of the essay may have been the desire to pacify Schiller after their acrimonious correspondence on Goethe. He may also, on reflection, have considered the reference to Iphigenie too cryptic. It remains, nonetheless, a perceptive remark. Faust stands as much in need of the support of a benevolent higher power in the working out of his problem as Iphigenie does in her own.

While Schiller fell behind Fichte in failing to appreciate the transcendental side of the work, he yet, perhaps unwittingly, encouraged Goethe to adopt for *Faust* the very solution he had rejected for *Wilhelm Meisters Lehrjahre*. In reply to the letter of June, 1797, announcing the resumption of work on *Faust*, Schiller pointed to the symbolical significance of the action: "So viel bemerke ich hier nur, dass der Faust, das Stück nämlich, bei aller seiner dichterischen Individualität, die Forderung an eine symbolische Bedeutsamkeit nicht ganz von sich weisen kann, wie auch wahrscheinlich Ihre eigene Idee ist. Die Duplizität der menschlichen Natur und das verunglückte Bestreben, das Göttliche und das Physische

1 Cf. *Goethe*, XVII. (1955), p. 139 f. Schelling says of *Faust* in the *Philosophie der Kunst* (1802-3): "Aber die heitere Anlage des Ganzen schon im ersten Wurf, die Wahrheit des missleiteten Bestrebens, die Echtheit des Verlangens nach dem höchsten Leben lässt schon erwarten, dass der Widerstreit sich in einer höheren Instanz lösen werde und Faust in höhere Sphären erhoben vollendet werde" (*Sämtliche Werke* [Stuttgart & Augsburg, 1859], V. p. 732). This was written before the publication of the *Prolog im Himmel*.

im Menschen zu vereinigen, verliert man nicht aus den Augen . . ."[1] To this Goethe replied on the following day that he was returning "in diese Symbol-, Ideen- und Nebelwelt mit Lust und Liebe". There can be little connection between his acceptance of the term "symbolisch" for *Faust* and his own discovery of symbolism which he reported to Schiller less than two months later from Frankfurt, for the word does not carry the same meaning in the two contexts. In Frankfurt Goethe did not yet view symbolical objects as entities embodying an ineffable higher meaning, but as "eminente Fälle, die, in einer charakteristischen Mannigfaltigkeit, als Repräsentanten von vielen andern dastehen . . ."[2]

Schiller used the word in this latter sense in 1800, when he encouraged Goethe to continue writing the Helena-scenes of *Faust:*

> Das Barbarische der Behandlung, das Ihnen durch den Geist des Ganzen aufgelegt wird, kann den höhern Gehalt nicht zerstören und das Schöne nicht aufheben, nur es anders spezifizieren und für ein anderes Seelenvermögen zubereiten. Eben das Höhere und Vornehmere in den Motiven wird dem Werk einen eigenen Reiz geben, und Helena ist in diesem Stück ein Symbol für alle die schönen Gestalten, die sich hineinverirren werden.[3]

1 Letter of 23 June, 1797.

2 Letter of 16 August, 1797.

3 Letter of 13 September, 1800. On the genesis of the Helena-scenes cf. E. Grumach, "Aus Goethes Vorarbeiten zu den Helenaszenen", *Goethe*, XX. (1958), pp. 45 et seq., esp. pp. 55 ff. Schiller's phrase 'das Barbarische der Behandlung' can be explained with reference to his description of *Faust* in *Über naive und sentimentalische Dichtung* where he compares the drama with *Werther*, *Tasso* and *Wilhelm Meister* and finds in each of these works a contrast between the ideal world of the protagonist and the "nüchterne Gemeinsinn" of the opposing characters (Albert, Antonio and Werner). The same contrast, according to Schiller, exists in *Faust*, "freilich, wie auch der Stoff dies erforderte, auf beiden Seiten sehr vergröbert und materialisiert". (*Sämmtliche Werke*, Säkularausgabe, XII. p. 214). This description may have confirmed Goethe in his intention to refine the material and the characters of the drama, so evident in the composition of *Faust* after the publication of the *Fragment*.

It clearly agreed with Goethe's intentions to have Helena regarded not merely as a beautiful woman, but as a symbol of beauty. The Helena-scenes represent Faust's aesthetic experience, in the phrase of the Paralipomenon his "Genuss mit Bewusstsein". In the structure of the drama as a whole this experience is ultimately significant because it is at the same time the result of Faust's entry into "ein bestimmtes tätiges Leben" and the preparation for an extension of this activity. The function of his aesthetic education is in some, but not all respects similar to that which Schiller explained in *Briefe über die ästhetische Erziehung des Menschen*.[1]

As long ago as 1896 Collin rightly pointed to "Genuss und Tat" as "die grossen Gegensätze, die in Fausts Leben miteinander ringen sollen".[2] Yet the contrast is not absolute. Faust's ultimate "Tat", if "Tat" it is, cannot be divorced from his sense of enjoyment:

> Im Vorgefühl von solchem hohen Glück
> Geniess' ich jetzt den höchsten Augenblick.

The trend of Faust's "Streben", viewed in the perspective of the whole work, is directed towards the extension and the refinement of his capacity for enjoyment within activity. He does progress from "der Dumpfheit Leidenschaft" to "Tatengenuss nach aussen" and "Genuss mit Bewusstsein". It remains to be discussed whether he also achieves "Schöpfungsgenuss von innen", (the last stage of his development adumbrated in the Paralipomenon) and whether Schiller had any share in marking out this ultimate goal of his "Streben".

What did Goethe mean by the arresting phrase "Schöpfungsgenuss von innen"? Emil Staiger explains: "das dürfte der Weisheit letzten Schluss umreissen: Faust,

1 Cf. H. Rickert, *Goethes Faust* (Tübingen, 1932) pp. 389-391.

2 J. Collin, *Goethes Faust in seiner ältesten Gestalt* (Frankfurt a.M., 1896), p. 158.

der endlich dazu gelangt ist, schaffender Spiegel der Gottheit zu sein".[1] It also appears to be a correlative of that "reine Tätigkeit" to which Faust aspires:

Ich fühle mich bereit
Auf neuer Bahn den Äther zu durchdringen
Zu neuen Sphären reiner Tätigkeit.[2]

The phrase "reine Tätigkeit" was used by Fichte and Schelling in works which were published in 1794 and 1797 respectively, at about the time when Goethe wrote the passage in which the above-mentioned lines occur. Fichte defines "reine Tätigkeit" as "diejenige, die gar kein Objekt hat" and "die Gottheit" as a being "durch dessen reine Tätigkeit unmittelbar auch seine objektive gesetzt wäre".[3] The difference between two forms of activity was explained in greater detail in 1801 by K. A. Eschenmayr writing in Schelling's *Zeitschrift für spekulative Physik:*

> Mein Geist und die Natur stehen einander gegenüber. In mir ist Freiheit, in der Natur Gesetz; insofern ich mich so erblicke, bin ich Spontaneität, Prinzip des Werdens, die Natur hingegen toter Mechanism, Passivität, blosses Sein . . . Insofern ich empfinde und anschaue, stehe ich unter der Macht der Natur, mein Vorstellen richtet sich ganz nach ihr, ich bin also nicht bloss reine Tätigkeit, blosses Prinzip des Werdens, in mir ist sonach auch ein von aussen bewirktes Sein, d.h. ich bin auch Natur.[4]

Much earlier Schiller had stated in *Briefe über die ästhetische Erziehung des Menschen:* "Der endliche Geist ist derjenige, der nicht anders als durch Leiden tätig wird, nur durch Schranken zum Absoluten gelangt, nur, insofern er Stoff empfängt, handelt und bildet".[5]

1 *Goethe* (Zürich), II. p. 323.

2 Lines 703 ff.

3 *Sämtliche Werke*, I. pp. 256, 263 n. Cf. Schelling, *Sämtliche Werke*, I. p. 390.

4 Pp. 6 f. Goethe possessed this journal in his library.

5 Letter 19. Schiller's formulation is clearly Fichtean, while Goethe is in close agreement with Schelling.

For human beings Goethe, too, recognized the equal potency of inward and external determining factors. It is the cardinal principle of his idea of "Bildung". In its sense he wrote to Schiller on 6 January, 1798, after reading Schelling's *Ideen zu einer Philosophie der Natur:* "Sie wissen, wie sehr ich am Begriff der Zweckmässigkeit der organischen Naturen nach innen hänge, und doch lässt sich ja eine Bestimmung von aussen und ein Verhältnis nach aussen nicht leugnen . . ." Beyond this knowledge lay the intuition of a realm where activity proceeds not jointly "nach innen" and "nach aussen", but with supreme transcendental exclusiveness, solely "von innen". That activity Fichte called "nicht-objektive, mithin *reine* Tätigkeit, Tätigkeit überhaupt und schlechthin".[1] The realm of such pure activity beyond the confines of nature, the scene of the eternally creative "Weltseele", is the empyrean to which Faust aspires and in which, according to the Paralipomenon, he was to experience "Schöpfungsgenuss von innen" after having indulged in "Tatengenuss nach aussen". It is the scene where the monads endlessly fulfill the divine creative purpose. The monads, Goethe told Falk in 1813 on the day of Wieland's funeral, participate "ewig auch ihrerseits an den Freuden der Götter als selig mitschaffende Kräfte . . . Das Werden der Schöpfung ist ihnen anvertraut". Here, too, "Streben" makes its quietus at last, for, in Fichte's words: "Im Begriffe des Strebens selbst aber liegt schon die Endlichkeit, denn dasjenige, dem nicht widerstrebt wird, ist kein Streben".[2]

Makarie is a singular personality in the body of Goethe's work in that she, if only partially and but passively, even in this life experiences "reine Tätigkeit". Unlike Makarie and like every other mortal, Faust has to await release from his "Erdenbanden" and the purging

1 Loc. cit., I. p. 237.

2 Ibid., p. 270.

of his "Erdenrest" before he can enter the realm of his highest "Genuss". He had aspired to this state of perfection long before his time and had learned to rue his precipitate arrogation:

> Ich, Ebenbild der Gottheit, das sich schon
> Ganz nah gedünkt dem Spiegel ew'ger Wahrheit,
> Sein selbst genoss in Himmelsglanz und Klarheit,
> Und abgestreift den Erdensohn;
> Ich, mehr als Cherub, dessen freie Kraft
> Schon durch die Adern der Natur zu fliessen
> Und, schaffend, Götterleben zu geniessen
> Sich ahnungsvoll vermass, wie muss ich's büssen![1]

At the time Goethe wrote the Paralipomenon, he envisaged Faust's ultimate participation in the scene of "pure" divine creativity and intended to conclude the drama with an epilogue on Mephisto in Chaos returning to hell. In the final scene, as we now have it, Faust crosses the threshold of the "Sphären reiner Tätigkeit", but is not seen to play an active part in them. The drama ends with his salvation and his purification. It stops short at the presentation of his final apotheosis. The only beings in the whole work who are shown in active enjoyment of the divine presence are the Archangels. In the first version of the *Prolog im Himmel* the Lord addresses them with the words:

> Und ihr als echte Göttersöhne
> Erfreut euch der lebendig reichen Schöne!
> Das Sein des Seins das ewig lebt
> Umfass euch mit der Liebe Schranken . . .

When Goethe replaced the phrase "das Sein des Seins" with "das Werdende", he did so in conformity with his own profoundest convictions on the nature of the universe in which he was confirmed by some of Schelling's writings that appeared at the time he composed the later versions of the *Prolog im Himmel* and of the Paralipomenon.

1 Lines 614 ff.

He could have found confirmation, too, in at least one of Schiller's works, a work, moreover, that was being completed in the first phase of their friendship. Phrased in the terms of a different school of thought, Schiller's definition of the essence of divinity in the eleventh letter on aesthetic education can help to explain one of the leading ideas presented in *Faust:* "Person und Zustand—das Selbst und seine Bestimmungen—die wir uns in dem notwendigen Wesen als eins und dasselbe denken, sind ewig zwei in dem endlichen . . . In dem absoluten Subjekt allein beharren mit der Persönlichkeit auch alle ihre Bestimmungen, weil sie aus der Persönlichkeit fliessen." It would be foolish to seek an influence here and vain to assert complete congruity. Nor had Schiller the ability to transmute his undeniably arresting thought into the matchless poetry of the *Prolog im Himmel* and the final scene of *Faust.* But over a wide area of discussion and correspondence agreements may be found which left their trace in Goethe's composition of his masterpiece.

REFLECTIONS AFTER TRANSLATING SCHILLER'S *LETTERS ON THE AESTHETIC EDUCATION OF MAN*

By Elizabeth M. Wilkinson

If on this auspicious occasion Professor Willoughby and I are looking more than usually hollow-eyed and sunken-cheek'd, it is because for a year and more we have been wrestling with a translation of Schiller's *Aesthetic Letters*, juggling with possible English equivalents for *Vernunft* and *Verstand*, *Geist* and *Gefühl*, *Sinne* and *Affekt*, for *sinnliche Natur*, *sittliche Natur*, *Notwendigkeit* and *Willkür*, for *Bestimmung*, *Bestimmtheit*, *Bestimmbarkeit* and *Bestimmungslosigkeit*, to say nothing of such innocent-seeming little words as *gemein* and *bloss*—one could write a whole treatise on Schiller's use of this latter word alone—for *Freiheit* and *Natur*, *Idee* and *Form*, *Stoff*, *Gehalt* and *Gestalt*, for *Täuschung* and, of course, for *Schein*. *Schein*! Some of you will not need a second guess to discover what we took as our theme-song, to cheer each other when spirits flagged; and at the risk of lowering the tone of bicentennial celebrations I shall sing it for you—first exhorting those amongst you who followed a now famous controversy[1] on the meaning of *scheint* in Mörike's *Auf eine Lampe* to ponder, as I sing, the multiple meanings of 'shine' in *this* context!

[1] In correspondence between Emil Staiger and Martin Heidegger, *Trivium*, IX, 1 (reprinted in *Die Kunst der Interpretation: Studien zur deutschen Literaturgeschichte*, Zürich, 1955); Leo Spitzer, *Trivium*, IX, 3; Ilse Appelbaum Graham, *Modern Language Notes*, LXVIII, 5; and subsequently several others in various journals, the most important being Sigurd Burckhardt, *Wirkendes Wort*, VIII, 5.

If you're anxious for to shine in the high aesthetic line as a man of culture rare,
You must get up all the germs of the transcendental terms, and plant them everywhere.
You must lie upon the daisies, and discourse in novel phrases of your complicated state of mind,
The meaning doesn't matter if it's only idle chatter of a transcendental kind . . .

Then a sentimental passion of a vegetable fashion must excite your languid spleen,
An attachment *à la* Plato for a bashful young potato, or a not-too-French French bean!
Though the Philistines may jostle, you will rank as an apostle in the high aesthetic band,
If you walk down Piccadilly with a poppy or a lily in your mediaeval hand.

The source, for those among our overseas guests who may not be familiar with our national line in operatic wit: Gilbert and Sullivan's delicious parody on the aesthetic movement at the end of the nineteenth century, *Patience: Or Bunthorne's Bride*.

And patience was certainly what we needed in face of Schiller's more tiresome habits. "Mit e i n e m Wort", he will say towards the end of a Letter, e i n e m in spaced type for greater emphasis. Ah! you think, now we can relax. Now we've done our stint for the day. Not a bit of it! He's usually beginning all over again. "Mit a n d e r e n Worten" is what he really means. Or that maddening way he has of taking the reader by the hand, and assuring him that he is now rapidly approaching his goal, when in reality he's still miles away from it. Why the hell doesn't he get there? you mutter. And then those dread moments when he announces: "Resign yourself, therefore, to one more brief sojourn in the sphere of speculation"; or "But this will lead us away from the realm of experience and cause us to tarry a while on the naked and barren land of abstractions"—the very last thing the English language ever wants to do. My particular bugbear was and remains his mania for exactly inverse proportion: "Dieses Vermögen wird in demselben Masse unterdrückt, als man . . . den Charakter durch Grundsätze zu befestigen sucht"; or "so hört sie in genau demselben Verhältnis auf, Object zu sein als sie Macht wird"; or "er raubt ihr gerade so viel von ihrer idealen Vollkommenheit, als er von seiner individualen Beschaffenheit einmischt". This kind of thing is not only extremely difficult to turn into elegant English; it often, I think, leads Schiller to a distortion of the true state of affairs in the interests of linguistic symmetry.

But why on earth, you will ask, did we go on with the translation? There are, after all, three in existence,[1] the third done as late as 1954. The most obvious reason was dissatisfaction, even with this last. This, admittedly, contains nothing so incongruous as J. Weiss's rendering, in 1845, of the famous definition of aesthetic illusion, "Nur soweit er aufrichtig ist . . . ist der Schein ästhetisch", which became "Show is aesthetic, only so far as it is upright"! But it has other faults, ranging from sheer grammatical mistakes of gender and case, or confusion of near homonyms (*das Band* confused with *der Band*, *erstlich* with *ernstlich*, *wagt* with *wägt*), through misprision of idiomatic constructions—*ihn auf etwas weisen* becomes 'assigns something to him' instead of

1 *The Philosophical and Aesthetic Letters and Essays of Schiller*. Translated, with an Introduction, by J. Weiss, London, 1845; *Essays Aesthetical and Philosophical* By Friedrich Schiller. Newly translated from the German. Bohn's Standard Library, London, 1875 (reprinted in the Harvard Classics Series, New Haven, 1912); *On the Aesthetic Education of Man in a Series of Letters* by Friedrich Schiller. Translated with an Introduction by Reginald Snell. London, 1954 (reprinted, Yale University Press, 1954).

'refers him to something', *vertauschen mit* is so misconstrued that at a crucial point in the argument (III, §2) Rousseau's 'natural man' is made to exchange a state of social contracts for a state of freedom instead of vice-versa—to the misunderstanding of technical terms common in the aesthetics of the eighteenth century. Thus "die Wahrheit lebt in der Täuschung fort" (IX, §4) becomes "Truth lives on in the midst of deception", whereas it should, of course, read "Truth lives on in the illusion—or semblance—of art".

One of the most troublesome characteristics of Schiller's style is his constant use of demonstrative pronouns: *dieser*, *jener*; *der erste*, *der zweite*; *der eine*, *der andere*. The English translator, denied even the advantage of gender, is often hard put to it to make unambiguously clear to which antecedent they refer—if he is not, by repeating the noun, to make his style heavily substantival in a way that Schiller's is not. And if he gets them attached to the wrong antecedents, as all the translators on occasion do—even R. Leroux,[1] whose French version is far better than any of the English ones—then it can be fatal to the sense at quite vital points. Take the following passage from Letter XXII:

> Darin also besteht das eigentliche Kunstgeheimnis des Meisters, d a s s e r d e n S t o f f d u r c h d i e F o r m v e r t i l g t; und je imposanter, anmassender, verführerischer der Stoff an sich selbst ist, je eigenmächtiger derselbe mit s e i n e r Wirkung sich vordrängt, oder je mehr der Betrachter geneigt ist, sich unmittelbar mit dem Stoff einzulassen, desto triumphierender ist die Kunst, welche jenen zurückzwingt und über diesen die Herrschaft behauptet. (XXII, §5)

Schiller is here offering his own, highly characteristic, transformation of a concept which has been of prime

1 *Lettres sur l' Education Esthétique de l' Homme*, traduites et préfacées par Robert Leroux. Collection Bilingue des Classiques Etrangers. Aubier, Editions Montaigne, Paris, 1943. There is a Spanish translation by M. Garcia Morente (*La Educacion estética del Hombre*, Buenos Aires, 1941) which I have not seen.

importance in the dramatic theory of Western Europe, a concept which, in the shape of *éloignement*, appeared in classical poetics as an indispensable rule, was thereafter, in his reflections on the art of acting, given a psychological twist by Diderot, and finally, in his famous *Verfremdungs-Effekt*, politicised by Brecht. Schiller sees more in it than a means for achieving desirable—or avoiding undesirable—effects in the art of theatre. It is for him the very secret of artistic creation in any medium. The signs of it are twofold: the subduing of the raw material by the form; and the distancing[1] of the reader, listener or spectator. Let us see what the translators make of this.

The earliest (Weiss) left it beautifully vague by using 'the former' and 'the latter' without taking any steps to make it clear to which of the antecedents each refers:

> Herein then consists the art-secret of the master, *that by the form he abolishes the subject*; and the more imposing, assuming, attractive the subject is in itself, the more absolutely that it intrudes its operation, or the more inclined the observer is, to merge himself immediately in the subject, the more triumphant is the art which repels the former, and maintains authority over the latter.

The second, by the anonymous translator in Bohn's Standard Library—the one our students still consult, though it omits all those long footnotes into which Schiller packed some of his most interesting thoughts—bears so little relation to the original that it is difficult to see how it was ever arrived at:

> Consequently the true search of the master consists in *destroying matter by the form*; and the triumph of art is great in proportion as it overcomes matter and maintains its sway over those who enjoy its work. It is great particularly in destroying matter when most imposing, ambitious, and attractive, when there-

1 Schiller himself, in *Über Bürgers Gedichte*, used the present participle in this way, i.e., transitively: "Aus der sanftern und fernenden Erinnerung . . . "

> fore matter has most power to produce the effect proper to it, or, again, when it leads those who consider it more closely to enter directly into relation with it.

Schiller's philosophical writings may, in the eyes of some, be merely "idle chatter of a transcendental kind", but they're not quite such nonsense as that!

The latest rendering (Snell) reads much better than either of these—the only trouble is that the translator not only refers *jenen* to the wrong masculine antecedent, but *diesen* actually to a feminine one, so that the end of the sentence reads thus:

> the more triumphant is the art which forces back material and asserts its mastery over form.

This not only makes nonsense of what the artist actually does with his material in the process of creation; it entirely omits the notion of 'distance', of keeping the beholder in a state of aesthetic contemplation. Even Leroux gets his antecedents confused here, and has the artist forcing back his material and achieving dominion over the spectator:

> l'art manifestera d'autant mieux son triomphe qu'il l'endiguera mieux et affirmera mieux sa maîtrise sur celui qui le considère.

What Schiller really means by this sentence, which is so central to his whole view of art and artistic creation, is as follows:

> Herein, then, resides the true secret of the master in any art: *that he can make his form consume his material*; and the more pretentious, the more seductive this material is, the more it seeks to impose itself upon us, the more high-handedly it insists on making an effect of *its own*, or the more the beholder is inclined to get involved with it, then the more tiumphant the art which achieves dominion over it, and forces him back into an attitude of contemplation.

It should be observed that the mistake Leroux makes here, unlike that of Snell, is not of the kind we usually term *Sprachfehler*—though it is, of course, ultimately due to interpretation, or misinterpretation, of linguistic material. But it is the kind of 'mistake' that native editors and commentators can, and do, make too. It is, after all, only because he mistook the antecedent of *jene* at the end of the third paragraph of Letter IX that Wilhelm Böhm[1] was able to accuse Schiller of excluding science and philosophy from his ideal of culture. And if both Snell and Leroux feel it necessary at one point to reverse Schiller's meaning by the addition of a superfluous *nicht* (XXVI, §14), so after all did Reinhold Köhler, in the great Goedeke edition,[2] at another point of the same Letter (XXVI, §5)—and at the instance of a sixteen-year old Gymnasiast, if you please; a shattering thought when one recalls that Schiller's treatise is said to be beyond the powers of our nineteen and twenty-year olds to-day. Walzel did not adopt this emendation; but the explanation of the crux which he offers instead reduces Schiller's argument, quite unjustly, to sheer tautology.[3] And if none of the translators has grasped the meaning of that central principle of Weimar aesthetics to which I referred above, an emendation that von der Hellen made elsewhere[4] suggests that, if he had been forced to commit himself by translating, he might not have managed any better. I refer to the well-known distich

> An Gebildetem nur darfst du, Nachahmer, dich üben—
> Selbst Gebildetes ist Stoff nur dem bildenden Geist.

1 Wilhelm Böhm, *Schillers "Briefe über die aesthetische Erziehung des Menschen"*, Halle/Saale, 1927, p. 30.

2 Karl Goedeke, *Schillers sämmtliche Schriften.* Historisch-kritische Ausgabe. X. Theil: Aesthetische Schriften, hrsg. von Reinhold Köhler, Stuttgart, 1871, p. 371, Anm.

3 *Schillers Sämtliche Werke.* Säkular-Ausgabe, XII: Philosophische Schriften, Mit Einleitung und Anmerkungen von Oskar Walzel, p. 375.

4 S-A., I, pp. 144, 323. In the German version of this lecture (*Akzente*, Oktober, 1959) I inadvertently attributed this emendation to Walzel, who did indeed edit Vol. XII of the Säkular-Ausgabe, with which we have inevitably been much engaged, but not Vol. I (Gedichte).

Its point is surely this: whereas the mere imitator is capable of nothing more than exercising his skill by copying finished forms, the truly creative genius knows how to treat *even* finished forms — "Selbst Gebildetes" —as mere material to be fashioned anew.[1] Von der Hellen, like some advocate of 'do it yourself'—more probably under the influence of romantic notions of genius—thinks this isn't good enough for the truly creative artist! Surely he must invent even his material! Hence he emends to "Selbstgebildetes", in one word. Self-made? Home-made? In any case it makes nonsense of the creative process as Goethe and Schiller understood it.[2] What the artist *fashions* is his form. His material he *takes*—wherever he can find it: "Den Stoff gibt ihm die Welt nur allzu freigebig . . . " wrote that greatest of all "takers", as Klopstock called him.[3] Indeed one might hazard a proposition: the greater the artist, the more he takes and the less he invents.

* * * * * *

But picking holes in other people's work, pleasurable as it may be, could never have furnished the drive to continue to the end with this Herculean labour. That could only come from our long-standing and ever-growing conviction of the greatness of the work itself.

1 Since I delivered this lecture, a student of mine, Mr. A. F. Bance (in competition with the sixteen-year old Gymnasiast, but to better purpose!) has drawn my attention to the fact that *nur* in the second line of this distich does double duty, working both forwards and backwards, in a kind of *apo koinou*. It thus means: 1. to the creative genius even things already formed are merely raw material (which is the way I had always read it); but also 2. things already formed are as raw material only to the creative genius. The two meanings are obviously compatible.

2 Cf. my comments on this distich in " 'Form' and 'Content' in the Aesthetics of German Classicism", *Stil- und Formprobleme in der Literatur. Vorträge des VII. Kongresses der Internationalen Vereinigung für moderne Sprachen und Literaturen, August, 1957*. Heidelberg, 1959, p. 24 f.

3 Goethe, *Noten und Abhandlungen zum Divan*, Jubiläums-Ausgabe, V, p. 212.

Just as we felt most defeated or infuriated by the wastes of abstraction, we would come across one of those golden passages, passages which, as Carlyle put it, "shew like bright verdant islands in the sea of metaphysics". Take, for instance, that resounding indictment of the fragmentation of modern man in Letter VI:

> With us, too, the image of the human species is projected in magnified form into separate individuals—but as fragments . . . with the result that in order to get any idea of the totality of human nature one has to go the rounds from individual to individual . . . taking from this one his memory, from that one his tabulating intelligence, from yet another his mechanical skill, and piece them together into a picture of the species. With us it might almost seem as though the various faculties appear as separate in practice as they are distinguished by the psychologist in theory, and we see not merely individuals, but whole classes of men, developing but one of their potentialities, while of the rest, as in stunted plants, only vestigial traces remain . . . Enjoyment has become divorced from labour, the means from the end, the effort from the reward. Everlastingly chained to a single little fragment of the whole, man himself develops into nothing but a fragment; everlastingly in his ear the monotonous sound of the wheel that he turns, he never develops the harmony of his being, and instead of putting the stamp of his humanity upon his nature, becomes nothing more than the imprint of his job or of his specialised knowledge . . . Thus little by little the concrete life of the individual is destroyed in order that the abstract idea of the whole may drag out its sorry existence.

There follows a ready acknowledgment that mankind as a whole has undoubtedly benefited from this specialisation of individual powers. But Schiller cannot help concluding with the passionate question, which has become not a whit less burning in the hundred and fifty odd years that have elapsed since he asked it (it is one of the key sentences of Father D'Arcy's new book on *The Sense of History*[1]): "But can man really be destined to miss himself for the sake of any end whatsoever?" Human

1 Father M. C. D'Arcy, *The Sense of History: Secular and Sacred*, London, 1959.

beings cannot be the mere means to produce a perfect society in the future; they are not means, but ends.

The 'wheel' in the passage I just quoted is, by the way, a metaphor: Schiller is talking of the way in which the individual has been degraded to a mere cog in the vast clockwork of the State. But we can scarcely read the passage to-day without all the associations of the machine-age coming up in our minds: the production-line, the adding-machine, the button-pushing, and Chaplin's unforgettable exposure of it in the tragi-comic antics of *Modern Times*. This accretion of meaning with the passage of time is, of course, something that happens constantly with great poetry. A precisely analogous case would be "the dark Satanic Mills" in Blake's *Jerusalem*: and I recall a heated argument on the BBC some years ago between the poet, John Wain, and the literary historian, W. S. Bateson, about the legitimacy of thinking of the industrial North when reading this poem. As we shall see, this is not the only way in which Schiller's language in this philosophical treatise operates remarkably like poetry.

Or listen to that clarion call to find the courage to put intellectual Enlightenment into practice:

> Our age is enlightened; that is to say, the knowledge has been discovered and disseminated which would suffice to . . . dissipate those false conceptions which for so long barred the approach to truth . . . Reason has purged herself of both the illusions of the senses and the delusions of sophistry . . . How is it that we still remain barbarians? There must . . . be something in the disposition of men themselves which stands in the way of the acceptance of truth, however brightly it may shine, and of the adoption of truth, however forcibly it may convince. A Sage of old felt what it was, and it lies concealed in that pregnant utterance: *sapere aude*.
>
> Dare to be wise! Active courage is what is required to combat the obstacles which both indolence of nature and cowardice of heart put in the way of our true enlightenment.
>
> (VIII, §4-6)

And does not Schiller's awareness of the dangers of repressing our passional nature, his conviction that the sins born of rigorous moral principles may well be more heinous than those of the flesh, his shrewd thrusts at our tendency to project the ideal self within us on to other people at moments when all they are in need of is our comfort and our succour—does not all this read like some post-Freudian programme of education?

> It would be no less difficult to determine which does more to hinder and discourage the practice of brotherly love: the violence of our passions or the rigidity of our principles; the egotism of our senses or the egotism of our reason . . . How can we, however laudable our precepts, how can we be just, kindly, and human towards others, if we lack the power of receiving into ourselves, faithfully and truly, natures unlike ours, of feeling our way into the situation of others, of making other people's feelings our own? But in the education we receive, no less than in that we give ourselves, this power gets repressed in exactly the measure that we seek to break the force of passions and to strengthen character by means of principles. Since it costs effort to remain true to one's principles when feeling is easily stirred, we take the easier way out, and try to make character secure by blunting feeling . . . And this, for the most part, is the process that is meant when people speak of *forming character* . . . A man so formed will, without doubt, be immune from the danger of being crude nature or of appearing as such; but he will at the same time be armoured by principle against all natural feeling, and be equally inaccessible to the claims of humanity *from without* as he is to those of humanity *from within.*
>
> It is a most pernicious abuse of the ideal of perfection, to apply it in all its rigour, either in our judgments of other people, or in those cases where we have to act on their behalf. The former leads to sentimental idealism; the latter to hardness and coldness of heart. We certainly make our duty to society uncommonly easy for ourselves by mentally substituting for the *actual* man who claims our help the *ideal* man who could probably help himself.
>
> (XIII, §4, fn. §3-4)

Or, finally, that strangely moving passage which so outraged Ruskin—though I think he must have stopped reading before he got to the end of it—a passage which firmly prescribes the limits, and thereby ensures the legitimately unlimited power, of aesthetic experience:

> In the aesthetic state, then, man is *Nought*, if we are thinking of any particular result rather than of the totality of his powers . . . For beauty produces no particular result whatsoever, neither for the understanding nor for the will. It accomplishes no particular purpose, neither intellectual nor moral; it discovers no individual truth, helps us to accomplish no individual duty and is, in short, equally unfitted to provide a firm basis for character as to enlighten the understanding. By means of aesthetic culture, therefore, the personal worth of a man . . . remains completely indeterminate, and nothing more is achieved by it than that he is henceforth enabled *by the grace of Nature* to make of himself what he wills to make—that the freedom to be what he ought to be is completely restored to him.
>
> But precisely thereby something Infinite is achieved.
>
> (XXI, §4-5)

Would it not have sufficed to select such passages and to link them together with a paraphrase of the argument? We rejected the idea for what, to us at least, seems a very good reason. The longer we translated, the more we became convinced that this treatise stands or falls as a whole; that it is not just, as has often been implied,[1] a veritable gold mine for the educationalist, in the sense that nuggets can be dug out of it and the rest thrown away as worthless and obscuring dross. It is no part of our intention to deny the charges that are usually brought against it. What we *are* going to suggest is that if Schiller's terms are inexact, then it is no random inexactitude, if inconsistent, not an haphazard inconsistency; that if his thought is guilty of illogicalities, it is not therefore without meaning; that if the form

1 E.g., by Snell, *op. cit.*, p. 16.

of the whole is confused, it is a most intricately designed confusion; and that the overriding intention has a clearly defined—and also definable—character, which is apparent in the detail of the language no less than in the dynamics of the total structure.

Before starting on some of the linguistic details, a preliminary observation about the state of the language at the end of the eighteenth century. If Schiller, as has been pointed out, uses the word 'nature', for example, in at least seven different senses, Rousseau used it in almost as many, and so did most other writers of the time. The passion had not yet developed for trying to make language unambiguous by castrating it, assigning to each word one meaning and one meaning only. An author could still expect his readers to grasp the meaning of a word by attending to both the immediate and the larger context, to the interaction of word upon word and to the controlling dynamics of the syntactical structure—this was one of the functions of hypotaxis and the sustained period. Nor had the notion of a technical language for each branch of knowledge yet been born. This is especially clear in the field of aesthetics. Schiller will use the word *Künstler* of a watchmaker without adjective or any other kind of qualification (III, §4). When he uses it of a statesman, he usually says *politischer Künstler* or *Staatskünstler*—but by no means always. When he means what we understand by artist to-day he often says *der schöne Künstler*—*not* to be rendered by 'the beautiful artist'!—but he does not feel it incumbent upon him to qualify it in every case. He did not need to. The word was only gradually acquiring a specialised meaning, and he could rely on his readers knowing by other signs when he was using it in its newer, more specialised sense, and when in the older, undifferentiated one. Thus when he speaks in Letter II of the State as "das vollkommenste aller Kunstwerke" he is certainly *not* thinking of it as an aesthetic object;[1] and if Böhm[2] had known more about the language of the time, he might have saved himself the trouble of attacking him on the grounds that he was.

It is against this general background that Schiller's 'loose' use of terms must be examined. And the translator has not been at it very long before it begins to dawn on him that he is misdirecting his energies if he tries to find an English equivalent for each term which will then serve him in every context. This surely is the mistake Snell makes when he plumps for 'perception' to render *Empfindung* or 'shape' to render *Gestalt*. His choice may or may not be good in itself,[3] but the real fault is its consistent use throughout. In these, as in many other—though not in all[4]—cases, the only factors determining our choice ought to be the meaning of the particular context and English usage. For what Schiller is after is not, as Kant was, a clear distinction between the several faculties of the mind, an exact delimiting of their various functions, but quite simply—if simple it can be called—the dynamic interplay between the two fundamental aspects of human nature: sense and spirit, nature and freedom, finite and infinite, or however you like to call them. If you think of these as two houses—or rather,

1 Though he was, of course, playing (in a way that was possible only before the word became specialised) on its full range of meaning: from 'artefact' through 'product of civilisation' (following Rousseau's distinction between *l'art* and *la nature*) to 'work of art', and, no doubt, anticipating thereby the Aesthetic State of the last *Letter*. But I insist that this is not the same as assigning to *Kunstwerk* the special meaning that it has today. What Schiller quite obviously means in this particular context (II, §1) is that the "construction of true political freedom" would be "the most perfect thing ever wrought by civilised man".

2 *Op. cit.*, p. 8.

3 Richards, Ogden and Wood (*The Foundation of Aesthetics*, New York, 1925, p. 82) also rendered *Gestalt* by 'shape', but it does not, in fact, seem a good choice.

4 It is, f.i., otherwise with certain terms which Schiller himself invents, or defines on their first occurrence, and thereafter uses consistently throughout; e.g., *Stofftrieb, Formtrieb, Spieltrieb*.

as two branches of a single house now at war with itself, for Schiller states quite explicitly (XIII, §2, fn. §1) that the split in human nature is not primary—then we might say that his interest is not in the internal relations between the inhabitants of either house, nor in assigning to any one of them his proper function in the economy of the household, but only in the prevailing tension, the frequent clash and conflict, the never-ceasing possibility of reconciliation, either between the two houses as a whole, or between any single pair which sallies forth to do battle on behalf of the rest. What I am suggesting is that any one of the denizens of either realm (for we must avoid undue attachment to the image I suggested above) can in a sense do duty for the others; that in Schiller's usage the terms *Vernunft*, *Verstand*, *Geist*, *Freiheit*, *Wille*, *Gesetz*, etc., on the one hand, *Empfindung*, *Gefühl*, *Sinne*, *Materie*, *Zeit*, etc., on the other, are to a certain extent interchangeable. The operative words here are, of course, "to a certain extent". I know that I am exaggerating, grossly exaggerating, in order to make my point. I do not wish to imply that a single pair of terms would do for the lot, still less that you could replace the two series by X and Y. But I do want to suggest that it is misplaced when reading Schiller's philosophical prose to linger on any one of the concepts; to put the full weight of your reflection upon it, or execute ratiocinative gyrations thereon, in a mistaken attempt to determine the exact range of its meaning and the precise nature of its function. Whereas it was wholly and entirely appropriate for Coleridge in his reading of Kant to argue with him all the way down the margin whether "der Wille" is really adequately defined as "Reason in Action", what we have to do with Schiller, or at least a great deal of Schiller, is to get quite clear in our minds to which 'side' the various concepts belong, and then dash on regardless, and at speed—tempo is of the essence—trusting to the syntactical structure and the rhetorical figures, to the recurrent rhythms and contrasting emphases, to keep us right about the antics that the substantival entities perform. And with the exception of the odd, really difficult, crux, they will do so.

What I mean by 'interchangeability' will be clear from the following example:

> Ihr Geschäft [der Kultur] ist also doppelt: e r s t l i c h : die Sinnlichkeit gegen die Eingriffe der Freiheit zu verwahren; z w e i t e n s : die Persönlichkeit gegen die Macht der Empfindungen sicher zu stellen. Jenes erreicht sie durch Ausbildung des Gefühlvermögens, dieses durch Ausbildung des Vernunftvermögens. (XIII, §2)

In this passage it would not matter greatly if, in the first sentence, we were to replace *Freiheit* by *Vernunft*, or repeat the same pair of terms after *zweitens* as before it—this would, in fact, bring out even more clearly Schiller's favourite rhetorical figure, the chiasmus, and make little, if any, difference to the sense:[1]

> die *Sinnlichkeit* gegen die Eingriffe der *Freiheit* zu verwahren
> die *Freiheit* gegen die Macht der *Sinnlichkeit* sicher zu stellen

The thing *not* to do is to anguish too much over the possible significance of his having replaced *Sinnlichkeit* by *Empfindungen* or *Freiheit* by *Persönlichkeit*. It is far more important to get the *feel* of the two aspects of the psyche reciprocally holding each other in check, to grasp—in the fullest sense of this word—the equilibrium of forces which is reflected linguistically in the pull of the sentence in opposite directions.

1 Since the German version of this lecture went to press (*Akzente, ed. cit.*) I have had the pleasure and privilege of reading in proof Herman Meyer's article, "Schillers philosophische Rhetorik. Eine versteckte Entlehnung", *Euphorion*, LIII, 3, 1960, which offers confirmation (the more pleasant to us both in that we were moving simultaneously, if along quite different lines, to similar conclusions) of this and other points noted below. E.g., p 321: "Der zweite Hauptsatz bringt, bei Licht besehen, nichts wesentlich Neues, sondern variiert das Gedankenschema des ersten in kunstvoller Abwandlung".

My next example illustrates this "jeu de substitution"[1] again; but at the same time another feature of Schiller's language: the subordination of the logical to the rhetorical mode in the interests of an aim which for the present I shall leave undefined.

> Sobald man einen ursprünglichen, mithin notwendigen Antagonism beider Triebe behauptet, so ist freilich kein anderes Mittel, die Einheit im Menschen zu erhalten, als dass man den sinnlichen Trieb dem vernünftigen unbedingt u n t e r o r d n e t. Daraus aber kann bloss Einförmigkeit, aber keine Harmonie entstehen, und der Mensch bleibt noch ewig fort geteilt. Die Unterordnung muss allerdings sein, aber wechselseitig; denn wenn gleich die Schranken nie das Absolute begründen können, also die Freiheit nie von der Zeit abhängen kann, so ist es eben so gewiss, dass das Absolute durch sich selbst nie die Schranken begründen, dass der Zustand in der Zeit nicht von der Freiheit abhängen kann. Beide Prinzipien sind einander also zugleich subordiniert und koordiniert, d.h. sie stehen in Wechselwirkung: ohne Form keine Materie, ohne Materie keine Form . . . Wie es mit der Person im Reich der Ideen stehe, wissen wir freilich nicht; aber dass sie, ohne Materie zu empfangen, in dem Reiche der Zeit sich nicht offenbaren könne, wissen wir gewiss; in diesem Reiche also wird die Materie nicht bloss u n t e r der Form, sondern auch n e b e n der Form und unabhängig von derselben etwas zu bestimmen haben. So notwendig es also ist, dass das Gefühl im Gebiet der Vernunft nichts entscheide, eben so notwendig ist es, dass die Vernunft im Gebiet des Gefühls sich nichts zu bestimmen anmasse. Schon indem man jedem von beiden ein Gebiet zuspricht, schliesst man das andere davon aus und setzt jedem eine Grenze, die nicht anders a l s z u m N a c h t e i l e b e i d e r überschritten werden kann.
>
> (XIII, §2, Anm. §1)

In this passage Schiller first states that for harmony to be achieved in the psyche the subordination of the opposed drives must be reciprocal. He then proceeds,

[1] I borrow this term, at the last moment, from Victor Hell, whose article "Esthétique et philosophie de l'art: Eléments d'une théorie classique d'après la correspondance de Schiller" (*Etudes Germaniques*, Octobre-Décembre, 1959) also offers welcome confirmation of this principle of 'interchangeability'.

again by means of chiasmus—a double one this time—to exhibit this reciprocal subordination linguistically. But what always worries my students is that, having first stated the problem in terms of drives, he proceeds to exhibit the reciprocal action in quite different terms, in terms of the Absolute and Limitation, of Freedom and Time:

Schranken . . . das Absolute : *Freiheit . . . Zeit*
das Absolute . . . Schranken : *Zeit . . . Freiheit*

When, in the preceding Letter, he first introduced the two basic drives, he did of course define them, gave each of them a couple of names, assigned them to the two basic aspects of the psyche, *Person* and *Zustand*, and allotted them their respective spheres of operation, Time and Infinity, Limitation and Freedom, etc. If we have forgotten this, we could of course turn back and refresh our memory. But my point is that we don't need to. For Schiller now trots them all out again. The demand made upon us is not that we should have mastered one theorem or proposition before we can pass on to the next. It is rather that we should surrender to the rhetorical figures, and let them guide us as to which concept belongs to which side, and how the various couples interact. It would, in my view, be entirely misplaced to worry our heads too much about the logical steps in the argument—e.g., "denn wenn . . . so ist es eben so gewiss".[1] If we only press on as far as "beide Prinzipien", we see that these principles refer not only to the two concepts which follow the colon, i.e., *Form* and *Materie* (though this is obviously their primary reference); they also refer to all the pairs which precede it: to *Zeit* and *Freiheit*, *Schranken* and *das Absolute*, *Stofftrieb* and *Formtrieb*—and, indeed,

1 Cf. Herman Meyer, *op. cit.*, p. 320, speaking of a passage in VIII, 6: "Auf dem Wege der Suggestion und nicht—trotz der scheinbar kausalen *Denn*-Verbindung—durch begriffliche Deduktion wird der Kampf der Weisheit mit der Sinnlichkeit hier der Einbildungskraft des Lesers als die eigentlich grundlegende Gegebenheit aufgedrängt".

to all the pairs which are still to come, right to the end of the paragraph. At the second occurrence of *Zeit* Schiller threw in *Zustand* for good measure. This demands, and at the same time facilitates, the introduction of its counterpart, *Person*. This at first pairs off with *Materie*, but *Materie* then changes partners and goes with *Form*; *Gefühl* makes its entrance, hand in hand with *Vernunft*, and *Zeit* has meanwhile taken up with *Ideen*. It is as if Schiller were playing variations on a single theme, the theme of the reciprocal subordination of two principles, and any member of the one series seems to be able to pair off with any member of the other, regardless of whether it is its true opposite or not. Speed, as I said before, is essential in reading a passage like this, because the meaning resides predominantly—though not of course exclusively—in the swiftly changing relations between the concepts.

With my next example I have tried to make the visual aids speak for themselves.

> [Wie sich das Gemüt bei Anschauung des Schönen verändert]
>
> Dem Stofftrieb wie dem Formtrieb ist es mit ihren Forderungen e r n s t, weil der eine sich, beim Erkennen, auf die Wirklichkeit, der andere auf die Notwendigkeit der Dinge bezieht; weil, beim Handeln, der erste auf Erhaltung des Lebens, der zweite auf Bewahrung der Würde, beide also auf Wahrheit und Vollkommenheit gerichtet sind. *Aber das Leben wird gleichgültiger, so wie die Würde sich einmischt, und die Pflicht nötigt nicht mehr, sobald die Neigung zieht*; ebenso nimmt das Gemüt die Wirklichkeit der Dinge, die materiale Wahrheit, freier und ruhiger auf, sobald solche der formalen Wahrheit, dem Gesetz der Notwendigkeit, begegnet, und fühlt sich durch Abstraktion nicht mehr angespannt, sobald die unmittelbare Anschauung sie begleiten kann. Mit einem Wort: indem es mit Ideen in Gemeinschaft kommt, verliert alles Wirkliche seinen Ernst, weil es k l e i n wird, und indem es mit der Empfindung zusammentrifft, legt das Notwendige den seinigen ab, weil es l e i c h t wird.
>
> (xv, §5. My italics)

This exhibit is meant to illustrate three things: 1. the perfect symmetry of Schiller's periods even at their most complex; 2. the kind of help we may expect from the symmetry in determining the meaning of difficult passages; 3. the bringing into being of a "third thing", the *Spieltrieb*, which is, on Schiller's own shewing (XIII, §1), "ein schlechterdings undenkbarer Begriff, weil die beiden Grundtriebe, Stofftrieb und Formtrieb, den Begriff der Menschheit erschöpfen", but which does, nevertheless, actually manifest itself in experience through a qualitative change in all our being and doing. There are in this passage some twenty-five substantival entities, all referring to the activities or objectives of the psyche; *Gemüt*, as the total psyche, subsumes them all; the rest, as my first diagram shews, are arranged strictly in pairs:

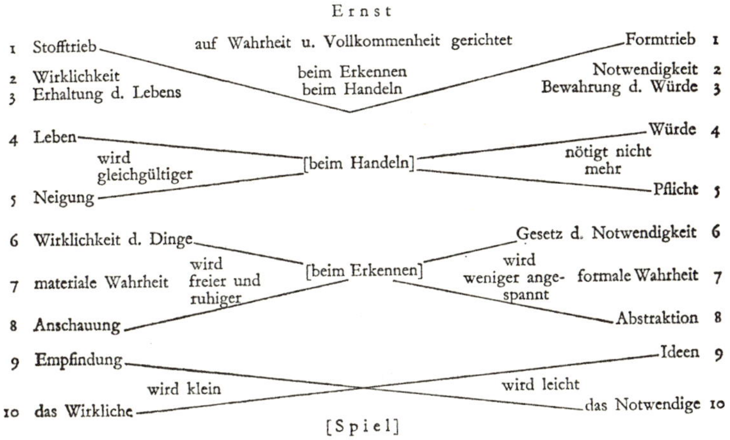

Concepts which are only implicitly there I have shewn in square brackets. For example, *Spiel*, which is the result of one aspect of our existence (*das Wirkliche*) becoming *klein*, and the other (*das Notwendige*) becoming *leicht*. What Schiller does is, first of all, to present the normal state of the psyche when it is involved in wholly 'serious' activity, whether this be intellectual or practical. Then, with the sentence beginning "Aber das Leben . . .", he begins to let the two sides of our nature interact and temper each other, first in the mode of doing, then in the mode of knowing.

The sentence in italics is one which has troubled interpreters. The notion of life becoming more 'indifferent' only makes sense if 'life' means, not the totality of sense and spirit, but life-serving activities in the biological sense. And, indeed, Schiller has thus defined it at the beginning of this same Letter. But even if he had not, its meaning in this context is unambiguous. For its pointing-off against *Würde* tells us quite unmistakeably that this is, in fact, its range of meaning here. We might, then, translate: "Life becomes of less consequence once questions of human dignity are involved"; that is to say: Dignity tempers the urgency of our self-preservative impulses. This being the sense of the first half of the chiasmus—for it's the same old figure again—the sense of the second half cannot possibly be conflict; it *must* also be tempering, tempering in the reverse direction. It cannot possibly mean: "Duty has no power to compel obedience when inclination attracts"—as though it were here a question of the Kantian conflict between duty and inclination. It *must* mean: "Duty ceases to be a constraint once inclination pulls *in the same direction*".

In the next diagram I have tried to make the symmetry of Schiller's period even more visual by reducing the concepts to a kind of notation (in which the small letters stand for nouns in apposition).

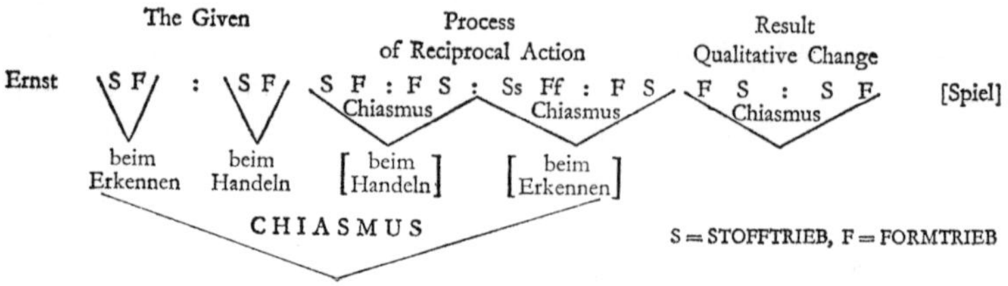

I am not, of course, suggesting that in order to understand Schiller's language it is necessary to draw complex diagrams of this kind, any more than to understand a piece of music one must first make an analysis of tonality and harmony. Here, as always, it is a question of learning the artist's idiom. This one does half consciously, half unconsciously. All I am trying to do by means of the visual aids I have set before you is to raise to full consciousness the processes by which we arrived at the meaning of difficult and obscure passages.

The mention of 'notation', however, brings me to a point already hinted at in my choice of metaphor. The dramatic character of Schiller's philosophical essays has been stressed;[1] and it has also been pointed out[2] that, if Kant hypostasizes the faculties of the mind, Schiller goes a step further and personifies them. This is, of course, true. Yet the impression left on *our* minds, even after such long and close preoccupation with the language as translation implies, is not one of sharply delineated characters. We don't really feel that we have got to know *Empfindung* very well, or that *Verstand* has become a close personal friend! They seem to us more like partners in a figure-dance, where the vehicle of meaning is not the individual character of any one dancer, or any single pair of dancers, but the evolutions which the various pairs simultaneously and successively perform. And has not Schiller given us the perfect image of such dynamic forms in his poem *Der Tanz*, where the "rastlos erneuten Bildungen", and the "Gesetz" which rules "der Verwandlungen Spiel", become a symbol of the unceasing movement in both microcosm and macrocosm, and of

1 E.g., by W. F. Mainland in his edition of *Über naive und sentimentalische Dichtung* (Blackwell's German Texts), Oxford, 1951, pp. 123, 129.

2 E.g., by S. S. Kerry, *Schiller's Writings on Aesthetics* (unpublished thesis for the Ph.D. degree, University of Manchester, 1957), p. 56. Cf. an article by the same author in *Publ. Engl. Goethe Society*, XXVIII, 1960.

the "Ruhe" which nevertheless "besteht in der bewegten Gestalt"?

What I am suggesting is that the measure of 'interchangeability' in Schiller's terms, tiresome, illegitimate as it may be from the philosophical point of view, has a positive aspect as well.[1] It deflects attention from the content of the concepts to the dynamic relations between them, and thereby offers an analogue of the perpetual process of the inner life, instead of encouraging us to think of this as a collection of discrete entities[2]—whether we call these 'faculties' or 'forces', 'thoughts' or 'feelings'. And it prevents attachment to names in order to fix our eyes on the psychical realities to which the names refer, inviting us to inspect our own experience instead of becoming bemused by the verbal apparatus of any particular system of talking about it.[3] It is almost as if Schiller were trying to prevent us making idols out of

1 Both were recognised as soon as the treatise appeared. A useful survey of negative and positive reactions in *Schillers Werke*, Nationalausgabe, 27, hrsg. von Günter Schulz, pp. 236 ff: 'Die erste Aufnahme der "Briefe über die aesthetische Erziehung" '.

2 I have since been emboldened to replace 'interchangeability' by 'tautology', and did, in fact, do so in the Taylorian Lecture which I delivered at Oxford on 17 November, 1959. This came about because, after hearing this lecture, my colleague, Mr. M. O'C. Walshe, kindly sent me his abridged version of Abhidhamma Studies by the Ven. Nyanaponika Mahathera (*The Middle Way*. Journal of the Buddhist Society, xxxiv, 2 August, 1959) who discusses the use of tautology in the *Dhammasangani* and points out its advantages for psychological theory. I cannot forbear quoting here the following (pp. 59 ff.) which, with little adaptation, might be applied to Schiller: "By the introduction of partly overlapping groups, the subtle and complicated structure of a moment of consciousness is indicated. It shows that a psychic unit is not "composed" of rigid parts arranged, as it were, in juxtaposition like a mosaic, but that it is rather a relational and correlational system of dynamic processes . . . Thus the danger inherent in a purely analytical method has been avoided".

3 Hubertus Lossow (*Schiller und Fichte in ihren persönlichen Beziehungen und in ihrer Bedeutung für die Grundlegung der Aesthetik*. Diss. Breslau, 1935, cited in *Schillers Werke*, N.A. 27, p. 373) is no doubt right in saying that terms which Fichte treats as purely philosophical concepts are for Schiller "wirkende Triebe". But this does not, I think, invalidate my point that it would be perfectly possible to become attached to the words in which such "drives" are talked about, and that Schiller's method counteracts the tendency to do this.

words, trying to make even a philosophical treatise tend in the direction of the art to which he said all the arts should in some sense approximate[1]—that art which, as he put it in *Über Matthissons Gedichte*, though denied the power of presenting the content of feelings, can with utter immediacy present their forms and the relations between them. "Diese Kunst ist die Musik . . . ihr ganzer Effekt besteht darin, die inneren Bewegungen des Gemüts durch analogische äussere zu . . . versinnlichen".

* * * * * *

But, you will say, and not without justification, how can a poet, a maker in words, ever be indifferent to any aspect of language? And, of course, there is a sense in which Schiller is not indifferent at all. If in his *Aesthetic Letters* he plays on the form of words—on *begreift/ergreift*; *Fläche/Flachheit*; *Form/einförmig/Formel*; *Säugling/Zögling/Günstling*—if he even alliterates and uses rhyming parallels, then it is incumbent upon the translator to find some equivalent of these formal relations in his own language. For this 'play' is meaningful. And Schiller knew it: his friend Körner,[2] for instance, would have had him replace *Fläche* by some such word as *Deutlichkeit*, but Schiller retained the cognates, though he was ready enough to adopt other suggestions of Körner's. If in the kind of case illustrated above consistency of terms was relatively unimportant, and substitution possible, in those now under discussion fidelity and exactitude are imperative. Consider the following examples:

> weil alle [Völker] ohne Unterschied durch Vernünftelei von der Natur abfallen müssen, ehe sie durch Vernunft zu ihr zurückkehren können. (VI, §1)

1 Cf. *Aesthetic Letters*, XXII, §4, which must be the original source of Walter Pater's famous remark in *The Renaissance*.

2 Letter of 11 January, 1795. The play on *Fläche/Flachheit* occurs in XVI, §3.

> so muss es bei uns stehen, diese Totalität in unserer Natur, welche die Kunst zerstört hat, durch eine höhere Kunst wieder herzustellen. (VI, §15)

Somehow or other one must find an analogue in English of the relation between the cognate pairs *Vernünftelei/Vernunft* and *Kunst/höhere Kunst*. It is essential to do so, because this movement of return—return to a state of primal innocence by the right use of that very same faculty, the wrong use of which caused us to fall away from it—is central to Schiller's thought. One might suggest:

> since all must fall away from Nature by the *abuse* of Reason before they can return to her by the *use* of Reason.

> it is open to us to restore by means of *Art* the totality of our nature which *artifice* has destroyed.

It is essential when reading the *Aesthetic Letters* to remember that each and all of the faculties, even Imagination, even the highest of them all, Reason, can—and do—go off the rails and cause havoc by mistaking their objective, and confusing their spheres of operation—by what Schiller calls a "freie Uebertretung der Natur" (XIII, §2): in which single phrase we have an example of the word 'nature' used in the widest possible sense—to include the mind of man and designate the law and order of all creation—and, at the same time, a reflection in language of this very process of going off the rails. For *frei* here is not, as so often, honorific, but pejorative: it denotes the *mis*use of freedom, and is probably best translated as 'wanton'.

But this 'return' is at the same time a progress. Again this may not be very logical. But psycho-logically speaking it makes very good sense. For the state of 'nature' we arrive at when we 'return' is qualitatively different from the one we started out from, different because of all the insight and effort it has taken us to get there. It is a state of innocence permeated with awareness—a 'second' nature. It is not, in Schiller's own words,[1] "diejenige Natur, mit der der physische Mensch beginnt", but "diejenige, mit der der moralische Mensch endigt". And we achieve it by learning to reconcile Nature and Morality, Sense and Spirit, Feeling and Reason.

We are, I think, much helped in reading Schiller if we bear in mind that he operates with more than one type of synthesis. It is not enough to say simply that the predominant structure of his thought is the synthesizing of opposites. It certainly is; but he achieves this in different ways, and again I have tried to shew it diagrammatically. The first type is the most familiar: the term at the apex of the triangle is different from either of those at the base, or else it contains them both:

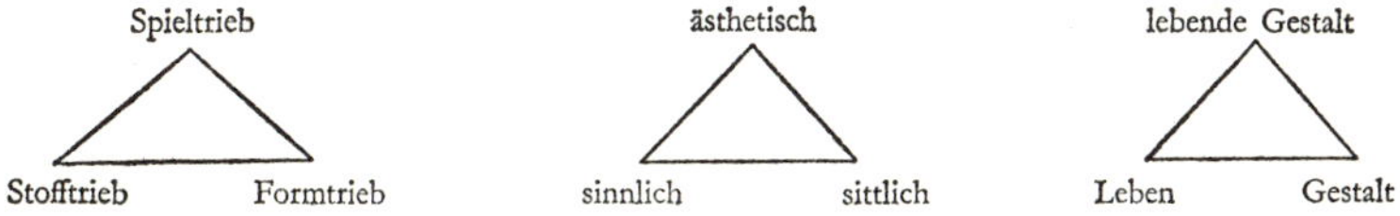

In the second type a single concept is polarised by qualifying adjectives. For example, Necessity:

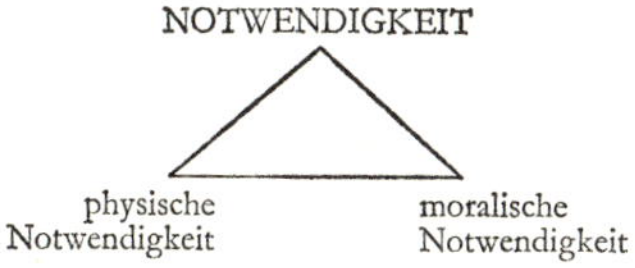

When, through the exercise of Reason, man succeeds in harmonizing the two aspects of Necessity to which he is heir, then, through insight into, and acceptance of, the great laws of Necessity which govern the universe, he achieves true Freedom. In this case the term at the apex of the triangle turns into its opposite: "aus der Einheit jener beiden Notwendigkeiten ging ihnen [den Griechen] erst die wahre Freiheit hervor" (xv, §9):

[1] In *Über Matthissons Gedichte.*

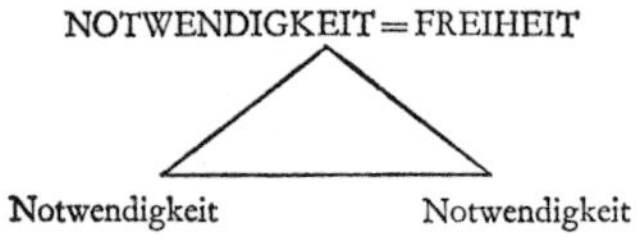

But the third type, Schiller's favourite, was, to me at least, known only from Goethe (though, as Schiller implies in the first footnote of Letter XIII, it is also Fichtean) until, a month or two ago, I encountered it in one of the recent books on Zen Buddhism.[1] There on the page before me were triangles similar to those I had exhibited in a lecture on the structure of Goethe's thinking delivered in Amsterdam and Tübingen several years ago:

In this type the term at the apex is the same as one of those at the base—but it is printed in capitals to indicate that it is a higher concept, embracing both the limited concept of the same name and its opposite. The mark, and the advantage, of this type of synthesis is that either of the terms at the base can move to the top, according to how you look at the matter. If, for example, in thinking of the synthesis of Nature and Freedom, or of Nature and Reason, our attention is centred chiefly on the state of grace in which man finds himself once he has achieved it, we shall put Nature to the top, in capitals because it signifies that higher nature, 'second' nature, of which we spoke above. But if we let our minds dwell rather on all the effort of Reason and Will that

1 By Hubert Benoit, *The Supreme Doctrine*, London, 1955.

have gone to its achieving, then we shall be inclined to shift the opposite concept to the apex in order to emphasise the triumph of the human spirit.

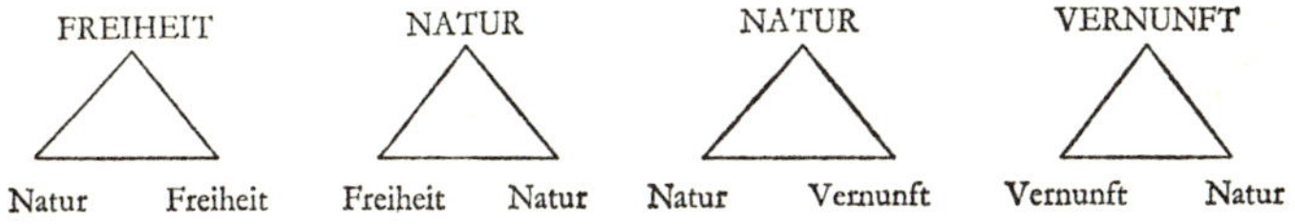

By bearing this in mind we can see the point of some of the alleged inconsistencies in Schiller's thought. In the first paragraph of Letter III he says that what makes man Man is that he does not stop short at what nature made of him, but has the power of raising himself, by his free choice, from physical necessity to moral necessity—that is to say, of transforming nature into morality. In the first paragraph of Letter IV he says what seems like the exact opposite: it is enjoined upon man to ensure that his moral behaviour can be counted on with the same certainty that we count on natural laws—that is to say, he is to transform morality into nature. Can he have forgotten from one Letter to the next? Of course not! The symmetrical positioning of the two statements—at the beginning of adjacent Letters—should warn us against jumping to any such conclusion. He is operating here with the perspectivism I have just described in connexion with the third type of synthesis, a perspectivism which he implicitly acknowledges as his method when, in that same Letter IV (§3), he looks at one and the same question first from the point of view of "der einseitigen moralischen Schätzung", and then from that of "der vollständigen anthropologischen Schätzung". In the last few Letters, where he deals with the tricky relations between the aesthetic and the moral, this perspectivism becomes the crucial principle of his thinking. If, as critics have complained,[1] he puts now the one, now the other at the top of his scale of values, treats the aesthetic now as means, now as end, it is because he is not operating with a fixed hierarchy at all, but with one that changes with changing perspective.[2] If the aesthetic is itself the result of reconciling our physical with our moral nature (a synthesis of the first type), it subsequently enters into a relation with the moral which is that of reciprocal subordination, and which gives rise to syntheses which can only be understood by reference to some such schema as Type III (p. 72 f. above).

Some of the features I have noted in the details of the language are also features of the total structure of the work. If there is a measure of indifference in Schiller's use of terms and concepts, there is also a certain indifference in him as to their origin. He will borrow from Fichte as well as from Kant, from Herder as from Rousseau, from Shaftesbury and from Baumgarten—to say nothing of the staple sources which nourish his mind: Classical Antiquity, the Bible and the Pietists of his native Swabia. As he says in Letter I, what he is really concerned with

1 Snell, f.i. (*op. cit.*, p. 15), thinks it impossible "to defend Schiller against the charge of an absolutely central inconsistency . . . He is presenting, at the same time, a Three Levels theory of aesthetic development, and a Synthesis theory—and he is mixing them up". I think Schiller knew perfectly well what he was doing, and if we accept, together with his principle of reciprocal subordination and his flexible hierarchy, this third type of synthesis, then he is seen to be perfectly consistent. As Benno von Wiese implies (in his edition of the *Aesthetische Briefe*, Im Scherpe-Verlag, Krefeld, 1948, p. 115), the double function of the adjective in the title indicates at the outset that the aesthetic is going to be both means and end: "das heisst Erziehung durch das Schöne oder Erziehung zum Schönen".

2 Clearly Schiller, like most poets, was adept at changing his viewpoint; not in the bad sense that he was too flabby to have any convictions, but in the good sense that he was flexible enough to see that the context is all-important, and that the 'truth' usually embraces opposites. A good illustration is provided by the titles of two of his essays which appeared within three months of each other in *Die Horen* (Heft 11, 1795, Heft 3, 1796), and were obviously meant to be complementary to each other: *Über die Gefahr aesthetischer Sitten* and *Über den moralischen Nutzen aesthetischer Sitten*.

are the "verjährten Aussprüche[1] der gemeinen Vernunft", not the particular "technical form" they have received in divers places and at sundry times. And if, in the individual paragraph, logic, though not absent, is subordinated to the X-form of his favourite rhetorical figure, so, in the larger structure, the linear argumentation is subordinated to a circular movement which permits him to play variations on his theme "im Grossen" as we have seen him doing it "im Kleinen". The tripartite structure of the treatise is obvious. But it is astonishing to observe, when one looks more closely, just how symmetrically he has placed successive elaborations of the same point. He covers the same ground in all six times, each time in different terms: in terms of the contemporary political and social State; in terms of the history of culture; in terms of the structure of the psyche, of the modality of the psyche, of a mythology of individual and racial development—coming back finally to his beginnings, but at a higher level, by treating of the Ideal State.

And this prevailing circularity of structure corresponds to the essential circularity of the main problem as formulated by Schiller himself at the end of the eighth, and the beginning of the ninth, Letter. Somehow enlightenment of the mind must be made to work back upon character. But does it not in a sense also proceed from character? Which is here cause, which effect? "Ist hier nicht vielleicht ein Zirkel?" he asks. For how are we to become wise if we do not already love wisdom? Yet how can we love wisdom unless we are already wise? They are, at the same time and reciprocally, cause *and* effect.[2]

But is not such close correspondence of form and

1 We have preferred *Aussprüche*, as in *Die Horen* and in the *Kleinere prosaische Schriften* of 1801, to *Ansprüche*, adopted by Körner for his edition of the *Werke*, 1813, and followed in most modern editions, e.g., by Walzel in Säkular-Ausgabe, and von Wiese, *ed. cit.*

2 A principle of his thinking, which, however, he does not state in so many words until Letter xxv, §5.

content a feature of poetry? Indeed it is. And ever since Schiller told Goethe[1] that the poet in him tended to get in the way when he was philosophizing, critics have been only too ready to attribute shortcomings in his philosophical writings to this intrusion. But some of them must have very odd notions about poetry, for they see signs of it in strange, even absurd, things: in the unsystematicness of his thought, in the looseness of his language (since when have poets been in the habit of using language loosely?), in the fervour with which he pleads the cause of beauty (this would make any eloquent critic into a poet!). C. G. Jung[2] even thinks it a sign of the poet taking over when Schiller, at the end of Letter x, abandons the empirical for the transcendental method, rejecting as a possible criterion of the value of aesthetic education any art that actually exists, in favour of the Idea of Beauty, beauty as an Imperative. But this would make Henry Home and Immanuel Kant into poets too! Surely the mark of the poet is rather in features such as those I have mentioned: a tendency to make form coincide with content, to exploit the sound-look[3] of words as well as their meaning, to make meaning to some extent dependent on internal relations, to make linguistic structures analogues of the psychical processes referred to?

All the same this treatise obviously isn't poetry. And not just because it isn't in verse.[4] Again we need to exercise caution in the kind of reasons we adduce. It is not just because this language relies on concepts rather

1 In the letter of 31 August, 1794.

2 In *Psychological Types*. Trsl. by H. Godwin Baynes, London, 1933, p. 111.

3 The term used by Elisabeth Sewell in *The Structure of Poetry*, Cambridge, 1952.

4 Though L. Urlichs (*Deutsche Rundschau*, VIII, 378, IX, 493, cited by K. Breul, *Zeitschrift für deutsches Altertum*, XXVIII, 1884, p. 358.) pointed out long ago how much more frequently Schiller falls into dactylic rhythms in the published treatise than he had done in his letters to the Duke of Augustenburg, and how easily they could be turned into distichs.

than on metaphors, on statement rather than on evocation. So does our own Augustan poetry; and the Psalms have been beautifully described as "a grave dance of concepts".[1] Nor is it because Schiller employs so much argumentation. So do our Metaphysical poets, to say nothing of Shakespeare, and not only in his Sonnets. Nor yet is it because of his fondness for rhetorical figures—Goethe's *Erlkönig* is compounded of them (by which I do not mean to imply that it is a rhetorical poem!) No! What makes Schiller's *Aesthetic Letters* utterly different from poetry, despite the presence in them of poetical modes, is their overall intention. Certainly they are, as Schiller put it in an undespatched letter to Fichte,[2] designed to engage the total psyche of the reader:

> Meine beständige Tendenz ist, neben der Untersuchung selbst das Ensemble der Gemütskräfte zu beschäftigen, und soviel möglich auf alle zugleich zu wirken. Ich will also nicht bloss meine Gedanken dem andern deutlich machen, sondern ihm zugleich meine ganze Seele übergeben, und auf seine sinnlichen Kräfte wie auf seine geistigen wirken.

And certainly that does sound very like the effect of art as Schiller himself defined it. But everything depends on our interpretation of the word *wirken*—and on our giving due weight to the preposition *neben* and to the adverb *zugleich* (second occurrence).[3] For it is equally certain

1 By Reid MacCallum in *Imitation and Design*, Toronto, 1953, p. 67.

2 3 August, 1795.

3 In *Letter* xxv, §5, Schiller contrasts the aesthetic effect of Truth with the aesthetic effect of Beauty: In the former we distinguish very exactly understanding from feeling, and feeling may well be absent without knowledge thereby ceasing to be knowledge, or Truth being any the less true. But in the case of Beauty it would be idle to try to distinguish them. There is here no question of either *nebeneinander* or *nacheinander*: feeling and understanding are so interfused that we seem to apprehend the beautiful object directly with our feeling. Now Schiller would, presumably, have maintained that the truths proposed by his treatise on aesthetic education remain true even if our feeling is not engaged by them. What I take him to mean by this letter to Fichte is that truths are to be conveyed, a 'message' transmitted, but that, *in addition to this and at the same time*, the total psyche of the reader is to be engaged. This is certainly not identical with the effect of art and poetry as he defines it in this treatise.

that these Letters are not meant to leave the reader in the aesthetic state as Schiller described it in the famous passage I read out earlier (xxi, §4), not meant to leave him without bias in any particular direction—freed and enabled, indeed, to make of himself what he ought to be, but still needing directives from realms other than Art, from the realm of Truth and of Morality, to tell him *what* he ought to be. On the contrary, these Letters tell him exactly what he ought to be—and how he can become it. Their dominant tone is exhortation, their dominant aim practical: to bring about not only a change of mind but a change of heart. To this end Schiller uses many modes of language: argument to convince us of the truth that is in him; rhetoric to persuade us to accept it; and something very akin to poetry to make it manifest, to *show* us what the change of quality he would advocate is actually like. If we do not recognise these various modes when we meet them, or if we mistake the dominant intention of the whole, then we come to the work with the wrong expectations, and are inevitably disappointed or exasperated.[1]

This work is, then, something of a hybrid. But is it a hybrid peculiar to Schiller? The answer must be a firm No! It stands in the grand tradition of doctrines for the attaining of true wisdom and the realisation of the psyche. Its ancestors are to be found among the sacred books, more or less mystical, more or less esoteric, of both East and West, its heirs among the practico-theoretical writings of psychoanalysis. Gerhard Storz[2] has drawn attention to its secularisation of Christian

1 This, perhaps, is why some people find Schiller's poems about art clearer than his writings on aesthetics. To them they spontaneously bring expectations that it is appropriate to bring to poetry: they are prepared to let meaning be determined by a variety of formal elements, and for logic and argumentation to be used for purposes other than those to which they are ordinarily put. Writings which have the appearance of philosophy, by contrast, they approach, and in some sense justifiably, with expectations of a different order.

2 *Jeanne D'Arc und Schiller*. Freiburg i. Breisgau, 1947.

doctrine, C. G. Jung[1] to its affinities with Taoism and other Eastern thought. What I am interested in at the moment, however, is not similarities of doctrine but analogies in the forms of thinking.

In method these *Letters on Aesthetic Education* belong to what may be called the tradition of transcendental pragmatism. This is to say, the truths they contain, though not arrived at empirically, are to be tested operationally: By acting on them, but only by acting on them, can we verify them. Like the books of ancient wisdom, these Letters can have no meaning for those not already prepared to accept what is in them. Like them, they operate with 'the logic of the illogical', with paradoxes that become fully meaningful only in practice: with the Way that can scarcely be called a way, since it never leads us as far as the Goal (XI, §7), and yet already *is* the Goal, since the Direction is already the Destination, and the Way is completed as soon as we enter upon it (IX, §6); with the method of 'Indirection' —that to go forwards we must first take one step backwards (XX, §3); with reciprocal or circular causality; with the notion of a third thing being brought to birth within us which is yet not a 'new' thing at all but rather a new quality in the use of powers we already have (what Schiller has to say in Letters XIII-XV about the birth of the *Spieltrieb* is, structurally speaking, exactly analogous to the opening of the 'Third Eye' in Zen Buddhism.) These Letters are like those books of ancient wisdom above all in the essential circularity of their main concern: How are we to become what in a sense we already are? How set out to find what in a sense we already have? Or in the words of Pascal: "You would not seek Me if you had not already found Me"[2].

1 *Op. cit.*, pp. 149 ff.

2 *Pensées*, VII, 553.

But, of course, we need not put it in religious terms. We might, for instance, put it in the terms used by Goethe in the last letter he ever wrote: How by taking thought can we learn to be true to that which is in us? How by conscious effort learn to move *with* the rhythms of our nature rather than against them? (a formulation of his life's endeavour which some critics—wrongly, as I think—find incompatible with his insistence that his growth was organic). And if we do put it in this way, then our minds are turned, gently but firmly, from the past to the future, to Schiller's affiliations with the procedures of psychoanalysis. I am not thinking now of the religious overtones of Jungian psychology, nor indeed of the content or concepts of any doctrine at all, but only of the basic assumptions and methodological implications of psychoanalysis in general as perceived by its most discerning theorists. Freud's debt to the Romantics has often been stressed. But it was after all Schiller who, provoked into disagreement with Schelling, formulated the poet's task as 'making the unconscious conscious': "jenes Bewusstlose aussprechen und mitteilen zu können . . . macht den poetischen Künstler aus".[1] It is true that what Goethe and Schiller understood by 'unconscious'—and the value they attached to it—is different from Freud's carefully defined concept. But what I am interested in here is only the *direction* of the process which all three uphold: from unawareness towards self-awareness. It is only because Schiller conceived the essence of art as a raising to consciousness of what was unconscious, through articulating it and making it thereby communicable—this is the true, if not always recognised, meaning of his *Aesthetic Letters*—that he could assign it such a vital role in the education of mankind.

[1] Letter to Goethe of 27 March, 1801. Goethe's reply of 3 April goes even further.

There are other structural similarities of thought. The truths by which psychoanalysis works are not arrived at purely empirically either; they, too, are only verifiable in practice. It, too, is powerless to do anything for the unwilling. Its concern is the discovery of the self we really are (not 'change' in any other sense), its problem how to convert 'I know' into 'I accept' (and am able to act thereon). Above all, in its theoretical explanations of how improvement—I hesitate to call it 'cure'—is effected, psychoanalysis has had to renounce the notion of a single factor, the simple linear conception of cause-effect, and fall back upon (or perhaps one should say move forward to) that of 'circular causality'. For until the ego is strong enough to bear the painful insights into repressed material, it will not be able to raise them to consciousness and integrate them. Yet such recall is itself a condition of the ego becoming strong enough for integration to proceed. Each factor is at the same time cause *and* effect, and they are best described as interdependent variables.[1]

What Schiller does in this work is what so many of the great eighteenth-century writers do: he works in a tradition and at the same time profoundly modifies it. And he modifies it by re-interpreting its symbols in new sets of terms—a variety of terms. For it is not his aim to gain power through words—any words at all—but to bring into the daylight of psychological understanding things which have a metaphysical sound, to open up esoteric wisdom and make it the property of all mankind (XXVII, §11). Pointing to the blend of Christian and Stoic elements in this work, Carlyle observed long ago[2] that it is yet without anything which even the most sceptical could designate as superstition. And this is

1 Cf. Ernst Kris, "On Preconscious Mental Processes", *Psychoanalytic Quarterly*, XIX, 4 (1950), p. 548.

2 *Life of Schiller* (1825), Library Edition, p. 135 f.

true. If, to take but one example, Schiller's allegedly indiscriminate use of some eight different names for the Godhead does, in fact, go back to theological polemics about Essence and Attributes and the Naming of God,[1] it also, and no less unmistakably, looks forward in hope to the time when men shall realise that, though the names they give Him be many, what they thus variously name is One and the Same. It is indeed "das alte Wahre" that is here "angefasst"—but it is, as Goethe said it should be, "noch einmal gedacht". The roots of this work may drive deep into the past, but its face is resolutely turned towards the future.

And if, in its concern with the integration of the psyche, it seems to look inwards, as though inclining towards a cult of the individual personality, it is also, from start to finish, a book about what Henry James called "the civic use of imagination". If, in its affection for the moment of aesthetic contemplation, for the instant suspended in eternity, it seems oriented towards the *vita contemplativa*, and attitudes we often associate with the East, it does also, in its insistence on the fruitfulness of this moment for the daily round and common task, in its demand that the freedom of spirit it affords shall serve the common weal, point towards the *vita activa*, and attitudes we are inclined to consider preeminently a feature of the West. Poised thus between East and West, past and future, individual and community, between the received truths of ancient intuition and the modern spirit of analytical exploration, Schiller's treatise *On the Aesthetic Education of Man* takes its place, alongside *Faust*, with which it has many affinities, as one of the greatest books in the German language. It is high time it was reckoned among the great books of the world.

[1] For another modification of this same tradition cf. my article "The Theological Basis of Faust's *Credo*", *German Life and Letters*, x, 3 (1957), esp. p. 239, note 51.

SCHILLER AS PHILOSOPHER OF HISTORY AND AS HISTORIAN

By Benno von Wiese

English version by Christopher Middleton.

On 26 May, 1789, exactly seven weeks before the storming of the Bastille, the newly appointed Professor of Philosophy at Jena, Friedrich Schiller, gave his inaugural lecture, "What is universal history and to what end do we study it?" Already famous as a poet, Schiller spoke to the students in that spirit of enlightened optimism which was firmly resolved to take its own century as the perfect example in no less a task than the vindication of history even before the incorruptible tribunal of reason. This was the Schiller who, in his great poem 'Die Künstler', written at about the turn of the year 1788-1789, had praised man as the "maturest son of time", "free through reason, strong through laws", "beautiful" man who with his palm-branch could stand "at the century's close" as a bringer of peace. In this light, did not all previous epochs possess a merely preparatory or, at worst, retarding character?

Critics of Schiller living in later and more skeptical times minimize his philosophy of history by arguing that it stands outside the great movement of "historism" which began in Germany with Herder and finally reached its peak in Ranke's great historical writings. They argue that Schiller never detached himself from the fundamentally unhistorical thinking of the European Enlightenment, and that he had no sense of the specific, individual and unique character of every historical phenomenon, be it a person, a nation or a particular cultural epoch. The idea of progress, as formulated in terms of reason, could not admit what was singular and irrational in history; Schiller accordingly remained, as a historian, a mere dilettante, who simply shaped the material of history aprioristically, in the image of his own preconceived ideas or of the rationalism of his age.

If one allows these objections, Schiller's concern with history must be thought rather fruitless—except perhaps as groundwork for his dramas. But this attitude is only one of the many prejudices in Schiller scholarship which are for the most part accepted unquestioningly. This does not mean to say that the time has come for a rehabilitation of Schiller as a historian, such as would relate his understanding of history to Romantic thinking on the subject. This would be a lost labour of love, or even a wholly false approach. Schiller does stand, once and for all, outside that movement which we now customarily call "historism". What we do need, however, is to revise our interpretation of the word "Enlightenment", and to use it no longer pejoratively but understand instead that Schiller's view of history and his way of presenting history, growing as they do out of the spirit of the Enlightenment, still have a positive significance, and that this significance has not already been annulled by history itself, seeing that Schiller's relation to the Enlightenment implies in many ways a criticism and a transcending of it.

For sure: Schiller does not, like Herder, refer back to a romantically transfigured realm of origins. He takes his bearings from the constellation of his own times and tries, from thence, to probe back into the realm of becoming from which this constellation arose. First let us examine this method of his as a philosopher of history. He realises that the tradition on which the historian must rely has gaps in it, that the filling of these gaps which make coherence difficult depends on a conception of history as a whole, and that this conception cannot proceed either from the accidental facts or from the causal connections between them. Another difficulty consists in the fact that world history as a whole is not complete, and it is, moreover, hidden away in the histories of individual epochs and peoples. The mere bread-and-butter scholar who does not concern himself at all with the question of history as a whole, cannot possibly arrive at a view of universal history. This view requires a "philosophical mind"; but even such a mind cannot appreciate the teleology of this whole (in so far as such a teleology may exist) merely by studying world history itself. We explore history empirically, and for this reason we can only consider it a possibility, but in no circumstances a proven fact, that a higher and purposive necessity guides its course. Yes, Schiller knew all too well that much in the course of history could give the opposite impression: the impression of a confused game without rules.

But where does the "philosophical mind" which Schiller considers requisite for the study of universal history obtain a guarantee for the progressive reason of the historical process as a whole? The answer is a daring one, and may at first seem to be an arbitrarily subjective one. "He derives this harmony from himself and transplants it into the order of things outside himself; that is to say, he introduces a reasonable purpose into the course of world events and a teleological principle into world history".[1] This demand is indeed far removed from that vigilant absorbtion in history which aims to understand how things have actually been, and for which every phenomenon in history—as in Ranke's formulation—

1 *Säkular-Ausgabe*. (ed. E. von der Hellen), Stuttgart, 1904-5, Vol. XIII. p. 21 (cited hereafter as *SA*).

relates immediately to God. The so-called "organic" view of history, as it developed successively from Möser, through Herder, Goethe and Romanticism, down to the historical school of Savigny and the brothers Grimm, does not fall within Schiller's field of vision. Instead, he regards history as a process still in the making, which must be determined by man, in that man decides to realize the reason of history from a source in his own freedom. Let us read Schiller's own words: "There must burn in us a noble confidence that we can contribute from our *own* means to the rich heritage of truth, morality and freedom which earlier times have handed on to us, and that we can secure our fleeting existence to this indestructible bond between all human generations".[1] This is not only the task of men who act in history, but also of the historian who desires to be a "philosophical mind". In that the latter understands history as the realization of a purpose, he himself collaborates with the historical process and contributes his indispensable share of the great task: a giving to human society of laws that are grounded in the freedom of reason. In this respect Schiller still considers the philosophy of history as applied politics.

Of course the way to this goal is very long and there are many obstacles and setbacks on it. Unlike Rousseau and Herder, Schiller paints a comfortless picture of man's contemptible beginnings. Reason has to be wrested from history bit by bit. Man, as we read in Schiller's posthumous papers, is not at first a reasonable being at all: "he only becomes reasonable late in time, and, moreover, when the order of the world is already established. Man is powerful, violent, he is cunning, and he can be clever long before he becomes reasonable".[2]

[1] *SA*, XIII. pp. 23 f.

[2] *SA*, XII. p. 326.

The way to human freedom, for Schiller, leads indeed, strangely enough, through the Fall, which he dares to name, in complete opposition to Kant, "incontrovertibly the most fortunate and great event in man's history". How is Schiller able to attribute such a positive value to the Fall as man's loss of the Paradise of nature? In his view, it was only through this event, with its symbolic meaning, that man was able to liberate himself from natural impulse and become a freely active creature and thus the creator of his own happiness. However problematic this happiness may be, it is founded only on man himself, and is therefore entirely his own responsibility. Man himself broke free from the "leading strings" of sheer nature, and "with his still feeble reason, still guided from afar by his instinct, threw himself into the wild game of life, took the perilous road that leads to moral freedom".[1] This is a revealing statement and sheds much light on Schiller's historical thinking: and I venture to maintain that his essential interest in history lay only with those events in which freedom in this sense played its "perilous" rôle.

But freedom, like all else in history, has its vicissitudes, and history is still far from being the history of human freedom. One may even say that the image of history projected by Schiller as a historian and a dramatist becomes—and not least under the negative impact of the French Revolution—progressively darker. Immeasurable are the hardships, the pressures, the failures, to which history shows man to be exposed in his striving for the freedom of reason. Schiller's presentation of history is corroborated in very large measure by one of the later statements of his Wallenstein: "It is the evil spirit, not the good, to which the earth belongs". History seen as mere actuality was for Schiller a part of the blind and chaotic working of raw nature, a world without order,

1 *SA*, XIII. pp. 25 f.

driven by the lust for power, by intrigue, ambition, sensuality, treachery, revenge and hypocrisy, a world of egotism and vanity, of deception and murder. Even heroism often sees itself caught in this double light, in this ambiguity of all that happens in history. In his treatise 'On the Sublime', Schiller's interpretation of history is pregnantly summarised: "The world as a historical object is at root nothing but the conflict of the forces of nature among themselves and with the freedom of man, and history tells us of the outcome of this conflict".[1]

Schiller's philosophy of history is thus far from being a mythical or simply idealistic transfiguration of history. Rather it was precisely his historical studies which gave him access to an understanding, without illusions, of the actual world of man and of the often hidden motives of man's conduct. On the other hand it is equally true that history remained for Schiller the process within which man makes himself man. In this respect he views history as a task, both ethical and political, which man performs, a task which makes it possible for man to become finally reconciled with himself, that is, with his conflicting natures, the sensual and the intellectual, and thus reconciled also with his fellow men.

The way towards this goal leads through human legislation. Schiller learns this primarily from Montesquieu. For laws regulate freedom, which at first anarchically and aimlessly insists on nothing but self-satisfaction, in so far as laws (to put it paradoxically) liberate freedom as a historical possibility and at the same time set freedom such limits as will stop the realization of its catastrophic potentialities. By limiting freedom, legislation makes freedom possible in a positive historical sense. Schiller's distinction between wrong and right

1 *SA*, XII. p. 277.

legislation is shown very instructively in his little treatise 'The Legislation of Lykurgus and Solon', which was written in 1789 and appeared in the periodical *Thalia* in 1790. This historical study has remained politically so explosive that the Scholls were able to distribute it as a pamphlet against National Socialism. In Lykurgus' legislation, the state dominated man in all respects; the legislator regardlessly sacrified the noblest and most beautiful potentialities in human nature to the abstract idea of the greatness and perfection of the state. However powerful and indestructible was the structure which Lykurgus aimed to create in this way, Schiller rejects it firmly, because the state must not ever be an end in itself but only a condition for the realization of human totality and freedom. Every totalitarian view of the state contradicts Schiller's idea of legislation, which aims, by limiting freedom, to make freedom possible as a condition not of anarchy but of morality. Let us hear his own words: "If a constitution hinders the progress of the mind, then it is wicked and injurious, however carefully planned, and, in its way, perfect it may be in other respects".[1] It is Solon's legislation which Schiller considers exemplary. For by it the very noblest powers of the Athenians were brought "into action"; he maintained respect for human nature and subordinated the state to the higher purpose: humanity. "His laws were loose strings on which the spirit of the people moved freely and easily in any direction and never felt that it was being guided; the laws of Lykurgus were iron shackles, against which the brave heart rubbed itself sore, and which with their oppressive weight abased the spirit".[2]

But how is it in modern Europe? Had not the French Revolution attempted to create by free choice the best possible state, that is to say, the reasonable state? Was

1 *SA*, XIII. p. 79.
2 *SA*, XIII. p. 99.

not the judgment of pure reason, and no longer the blind right of the strong, supposed to decide on a more just constitution? Yet Schiller's answer to these questions is negative. In his letter of 13 July, 1793, to Duke Friedrich Christian von Augustenburg, this is stated quite unequivocally: "If it were true that the extraordinary thing really had happened, that political legislation had been assigned to reason, that man was respected and treated as an end in himself, that law had been enthroned and true freedom made the keystone of the state, then I would say farewell to the Muses for ever and devote all my activity to the most glorious of all works of art, the monarchy of reason. But it is precisely this that I dare to doubt. I am very far from believing that a political regeneration has begun; indeed, present events rob me of all hope that this will ever come to pass for centuries".[1]

When Schiller delivered his inaugural lecture, free legislation by reason had seemed near; the French Revolution showed how far away it still was. Instead of it, the peoples of Europe are thrown back upon the conflict between freedom and terror. The task of man in the present can then only consist in his getting beyond painful submission to the tension between the start that he has made for freedom and the renewed stagnation and terrorisation which, paradoxically, springs out of it. For Schiller believes throughout that all peoples and states have a common responsibility to the idea of humanity. In his letters "On the Aesthetic Education of Man" he asks as a philosopher: "Why is it that we are still barbarians?"[2] Schiller's aesthetics are an attempt to answer this question, not only by giving an analytical diagnosis of his times but also by attempting to show

1 *Briefe.* (ed. F. Jonas), Vol. III. p. 332.

2 *SA*, XII. p. 27.

the way out of this barbarism. His later aesthetics are thus a development of his philosophy of history and also a practical and pedagogic application of it.

Schiller's first great historical work, *A History of the Decline of the United Netherlands* (first published as a book in 1788), was written before the French Revolution began. He never considered events in history as isolated individual phenomena, but saw them analogically in relation to unchanging human nature and thus also to the political situation of his own time. This is most clearly shown in his introduction (1788) by a statement written one year before the Declaration of Human Rights, though later omitted owing to his negative reaction to the French Revolution: "Thus the power with which it [the people of the Netherlands] acted has not vanished from among us; the happy outcome which crowned its most daring venture will also be ours when such times return and similar motives call for similar actions."[1]

In the introduction to his historical work, Schiller seems to be allotting good and evil onesidedly. On the one hand there is the people of the Netherlands, representing the idea of freedom; on the other hand the Spanish king, Philip, practises his policy of fear with "furtiveness as the godhead of his cabinet". But the conflict between the ideal purpose, with its human appeal, and Schiller's growing insight into the ramifications and complexities of human conduct, becomes more and more evident as the book proceeds.

The ideas in the introduction lead one to expect, in what follows, a triumph of moral reason in history, culminating in the victory of a free and authentically human people. But this is the opposite of what actually does happen. In the course of the narrative, the antithetic contrast of freedom and despotism is gradually

1 *SA*, XIV. p. 431.

abandoned. The work, which remained unfinished, does not culminate in the victorious liberation of the people of the Netherlands, but breaks off with Alba's forbidding arrival in Brussels, with the imprisonment of Egmont and Hoorne, with Margarete of Parma's abdication, and with the Duke's final instatement as Governor General. It is precisely the story-teller in Schiller who discovers more and more that history is concrete and complex and real. The dramatic pathos and the poet's sympathetic identification of himself with his hero yield to an objective understanding of the variable conditions and necessities to which both sides were subject. Thus it is that the people of the Netherlands no longer represent the cause of freedom proper any more than the Spaniards represent despotism and tyranny. As a historian, Schiller retains the cool detachment which he himself thought requisite; he leaves it to the reader to act as judge. He is not concerned to admit his own ideas into history in the way in which he did as a dramatist in *Don Carlos*, and even as a philosopher in the later inaugural lecture. The facts of history are left to speak for themselves. Even the enemy is entitled to justice from the narrator. Every historical phenomenon has its own light and its own shadow. Schiller obtains increasing insight into the mixed character of human nature and all its actions. It is precisely in his sublime and most subtly nuanced art of the historical portrait—whether the subject be Philip or Orange—that the great historical personalities become generalized individuals, whose powerful influence in history unleashes simultaneously good and evil.

Nevertheless certain ideas implying a philosophy of history are introduced even into the *History of the Decline of the United Netherlands*. This is apparent in Schiller's application of those categories which Kant worked out in his 'Ideas towards a General History' (1784) and

'Conjectures on the Beginning of the History of Man' (1786), namely the categories of the "economy of nature", the "plan of nature" and "providence". Of course, only the "instant" ("Augenblick") and the "point" ("Punkt") belong to man in history; of course, world history moves forward only under the pressure of "fortuity" ("Zufall"); but all the same Schiller leaves it in the balance whether or not we may consider history simultaneously as the outcome of fortuity and as the work of a "higher understanding". This naturally has nothing to do with that Romantic mystique of history which envisages all things as products of a mysterious suprapersonal subject of history and as the workings of its necessity. Schiller does not refer either directly or indirectly to any "Volksseele", "Volksgeist" or "Weltgeist". Rather it is typical of his attitude that, even where he is thinking teleologically in terms of a world-plan, this plan in its realization remains strictly associated with the political decisions made by individual men. The reason of the whole pattern is never something ready-made; it is a task which man has to perform. It is up to the individual who acts in history to decide whether or not he shall shape the given instant into the "plan of wisdom". Certainly he cannot envisage all the consequences of his actions; but it is enough if the forces and passions which gave rise to a situation constituted in themselves "noble forces, great and beautiful actions", and were thus not unworthy of the task "which they unwittingly served".[1]

In his suggestion of a "higher order of things", Schiller as a philosopher of history employs another category, for which he is doubtless indebted to Herder. This is the category of Nemesis. Herder had discussed the moral implicit in the metaphor of Nemesis at length in his *Zerstreute Blätter*, especially in the second collection,

1 *SA*, XIV. pp. 16 f.

dated 1786. Schiller is continuing Herder's line of thought when he speaks of Fatum and Nemesis and therewith recognizes that the incalculable element in historical events enshrines the secret workings of a pattern of laws and of a higher retributive justice. Nemesis is the idealistic antitype of the Baroque Fortuna. It does not, like Fortuna, function in terms of the purely fortuitous rise and fall of destinies in history, but has become rather a kind of court of appeal in which we can decide our own future for ourselves. To honour Nemesis means to submit to the higher economy of destiny; as Herder had put it "We carry Nemesis within ourselves", and "each man's destination is inscribed in his own being".[1]

For Schiller, nature in its vastness, charged with history, is the first condition for the entry of Nemesis into human affairs. Man is perpetually being challenged to intervene daringly in the historical process even where he is impotent to survey the full consequence of his actions. Schiller always considered history as the realization of human freedom, even if, as narrator of historical events, he shows less the inner pathos of this freedom than the constrictions which are always shackling man and holding him back. Yet it is possible for man to act, at certain points in history where the issues do not yet automatically involve compulsion, in such a way that his freedom of action inaugurates a new series of events. But the source of all action is the human heart, and Schiller, as a dramatist and as a historian, seeks to understand the heart as something which is as homogeneous as it is composite, in its relation to the continually "variable" external influences which condition it. For "in man's whole history", Schiller considers, "no chapter is more

[1] *Werke* (ed. Suphan), Vol. XVI. p. 374; cf. Herder's essay, 'Nemesis. Ein lebendes Sinnbild', ibid. XV. pp. 395-428.

instructive to heart and mind than the annals of his errors".[1] Man carries Nemesis, too, in his own heart.

The style of Schiller's narrative is also conditioned by this passionate participation in the human heart as the source of all action. One might have the impression, after reading what he demands in his inaugural lecture, that he would be writing a history of ideas; yet this is not the case; rather he prefers to concentrate his account of events in the figures of historical personalities. Yet individuals here have equally a suprapersonal significance; they are—if I may repeat the expression—generalized individuals. The interest of the narrator concerns man as an agent and those suprapersonal forces which he brings into play. The result of this is that again and again in Schiller's vivid narrative, the purely ideal conception that history conforms to the principle of reason gives way to those moments at which, from the heart's impulses, which may be hidden but are nonetheless analysed in their complexity with great psychological precision, the irrevocable historical actions spring.

Significantly enough, also in Schiller's second great historical work, his *History of the Thirty Years' War* (1791-93), the general ideas of "Emperor" and "Unity" play a very minor part, and even the conflict between the confessions is described in an astonishingly cold and matter-of-fact way. There is no question here of the account being tendentious, either in a religious or in a nationalistic sense. Instead, the two main figures, Gustav Adolf and Wallenstein, are presented in such a way that each elucidates the other; and this contrapuntal treatment of them governs the whole narrative. Schiller as a historian pays more and more attention to concrete figures and events rather than to abstract political ideas and religious conflicts.

[1] *SA*, II. p. 191.

However much the two great men, Gustav Adolf and Wallenstein, may dominate events, around them the panorama of history unfolds: great kings and weak ones, faithful chancellors, intelligent and cautious councillors, opportunists and tacticians, rebels and intriguers, fanatics and cowards, ungrateful friends and rescued enemies.

Schiller's special preference is not only for the two men of historical destiny, but also for the pariahs of society who do not participate in their small squabbles—those adventurers and generals like Mansfeld, Bernhard von Weimar, Pappenheim, Banér, Hatzfeld and others. Their freely choosing to stand above events gives them their disposition for greatness which might have brought them immortality. Let us take Mansfeld, the knight of fortune, as an example. His whole power lay in his sword: a usurper, whose very legitimacy was a matter of controversy to others, always persecuted by destiny, but always greater than it. Courage and force of personality are here worth more than possessions, and the early deaths of such men set the seal, as it were, on their decision to be free. Such characters may not have been rewarded with success, in history as a whole; but Schiller respects them for the courageous and free spirit which they bring into the world. Their very independence signifies moral power, because man here is seen to be acting not from vulgar motives, and not in accordance with mediocre and conventional standards of intelligence, but with a kind of aristocratic pride which stakes everything on the person alone.

But it is Gustav Adolf who is unique in his kind, a king who enters history as a bringer of light indeed. It is even given to this man, with his "lofty impetus", conqueror, legislator and judge in one, to die "in the fullness of his glory and with his name unsullied".[1] Thus he was and

[1] *SA*, xv. p. 213.

remained the one and only just conqueror. With such traits as these, Schiller created the popular image of Gustav Adolf as a knight of the evangelical religion and of German freedom. He even considered making a heroic epic out of the material, hoping thus to create a happy union of national and cosmopolitan interests.[1]

Gustav Adolf, hero and man in one, legislator and king, great-hearted and a just conqueror; there can be no doubt that Schiller loved and admired no other figure in history more than him. But here too the realistic psychology of the story-teller intervenes and analyses the limits of such ideality. In the concluding characterization of him—gently anticipated as it is, it comes as rather a surprise — — it is made quite clear why Gustav Adolf, had he lived longer, would have become an unjust conqueror. His ambitious desire to gain power in Germany would never, in the long run, have accorded with the freedom of the people. Gustav Adolf on the imperial throne, the foreigner who had grown up amid the principles of absolute monarchy: he would not have been, in Schiller's view, the right man "to guard the sanctuary of the German way of life, and to respect the people's freedom". So his death was the "greatest service that he could do the freedom of the German Empire".[2] For his death alone made possible the restoration in Europe of the balance of power which he had threatened to disturb.

As a philosopher of history Schiller interprets Gustav Adolf's death in terms of Nemesis. Thus it obtains a special meaning. Gustav Adolf respected limitation and balance and thus also the punitive Nemesis which sets

1 *Briefe*, ed. cit., III. pp. 170 f.

2 *SA*, XV. p. 317.

limits to any excessive self-exaltation. For this reason he received the favours of Nemesis even in death, because by virtue of his dying at the right time Nemesis prevented him from overstepping human limits and from being remembered not as the sole just conqueror but as one of the many unjust conquerors. Herein lay the metaphysical significance of his death: "The historian, whose work is often no more than the joyless business of scrutinizing the montonous play of human passions, is sometimes rewarded by finding phenomena which fall as out of the sky into the regular clockwork of human undertakings, and direct the reflective mind towards a higher order of things".[1]

"A higher order of things" is active, too, though in a different sense, in Wallenstein's destiny. Schiller was later to search repeatedly for a vignette representing Nemesis, as a frontispiece for his *Wallenstein* trilogy.[2] Of course it is here not the merciful but the avenging Nemesis which Wallenstein's actions incur. But Nemesis remained nonetheless that earnest goddess, the medium of tragic purification, who allows Wallenstein in death and through his death to achieve a greatness that he could not thus have achieved in life.

At first sight, admittedly, Schiller's account of the events in his history seems to represent Wallenstein merely as a dark foil to the light-bringing hero Gustav Adolf. Gustav Adolf had uncommon luck in that, right up to his death, his personal plans coincided with the plan of history—whether the latter be called the "economy of nature", "nature in her vastness", or "providence". Wallenstein, on the other hand, the sovereign lord of history, creator of massive power-complexes, becomes

1 Ibid.

2 See the letter to Cotta, 30 November, 1796, *Briefe*, ed. cit., v. p. 125.

inevitably the man who is doomed to fall, the man who is overwhelmed by the projects of his own power, and who loses his grip. Schiller speaks of him simultaneously with abhorrence and with admiration; he describes, after Wallenstein's deposition at Regensburg, his situation as that of a "criminal from loss of kudos", who became henceforth a thief because of the theft which he himself had suffered. What a danger this man could be to the Emperor when the latter, in his hour of need, had to recall him and give him unlimited power to punish and reward, and when "the proudest of servants dared to dictate laws to the proudest of princes!"[1]

But however dark and ambiguous Wallenstein's character may be in Schiller's history, however much his greatness may be only that of an adventurer who inspires "admiration" and "fear" but cannot compel "respect" and "submission" as "legitimate greatness" can, however much, too, his treachery against the Emperor is interpreted as an offence against a power that is sanctified by religion and law, nonetheless it is astonishing to what extent already in Schiller's historical account the declining Wallenstein has tragic grandeur. "He stands there alone, deserted by all those to whom he has done good, betrayed by all those on whom he has relied. But situations like these are the real test of great character. Deceived in every expectation, he abandons none of his plans; he gives nothing up for lost, because he still has himself".[2]

The concluding characterization of Gustav Adolf showed the shadow cast by this radiant figure. The concluding characterization of Wallenstein forms a further contrast, for here the dark image of the ambitious adven-

1 *SA*, xv. p. 275.

2 *SA*, xv. pp. 367 f.

turer brightens, being stylized into greatness. Wallenstein's life ends when he is fifty, an "active and extraordinary life; raised up by aspiration, flung down by overweening ambition, with all his faults still a great and admirable man, matchless, if he had only kept within limits. The virtues of the ruler and of the hero: intelligence, justice, firmness and courage, these his character displayed in colossal measure; but he lacked the gentler virtues of man which grace the hero and arouse love in the ruler".[1] Yes, finally the historian considers Wallenstein's treachery as unproved, and sees his secession to the Swedes as an act to which only necessity and despair drove him. "So Wallenstein did not fall because he was a rebel; he rebelled because of his fall".[2]

Wallenstein is thereby changed from a dubious character into a tragic one; he becomes a sacrifice of history itself, history which he had attempted overweeningly to subordinate to his will and which in the end, as an avenging Nemesis, destroyed him. The creator of history becomes a creature of history. The two generals Gustav Adolf and Wallenstein, who had originally been kept strictly apart like good and evil, are drawn in the course of the narrative imperceptibly closer to each other, moving towards each other, as was earlier the case with Orange and King Philip in the *Decline of the United Netherlands*. Both have greatness, both are rulers and heroes, and both stand under the law of Nemesis. Nonetheless, the one is the born and legitimate king, while the other is the illicit adventurer. Gustav Adolf had to pay for the union of purity and power in his person by dying prematurely, because this union would not have been vouchsafed to him much longer without his death.

1 *SA*, xv. p. 375.

2 *SA*, xv. p. 376.

Wallenstein, on the other hand, dies as a result of the intervention of a punitive justice, which ultimately catches up with all human actions. But his dubious life thereby receives a purifying significance. In both cases, as in Schiller's historical dramas, history in the last instance is a divine tribunal, even if we do not hear the voice of the divinity speaking directly, but only through the mediation of Nemesis, that Nemesis which the divinity has sent to us as its emissary and which repeatedly sets aright the injuries done to the limits which are imposed upon mankind.

At the outset we were concerned with Schiller's enlightened optimism, which aimed to justify history in terms of reason. But the more deeply Schiller pondered history, the more he tended to consider it as a complex reality which transcends any simple dualism of idea and actuality or even of good and evil. This attitude was fertile to his art, especially in the *Wallenstein* trilogy, in which the impenetrable, insoluble and yet strictly necessary character of all history was mastered within the economy of a tragic action. To examine this point more closely would however lead away from our present theme.

In conclusion one point should be specially emphasized. What fascinated Schiller in history again and again was the opportunity for greatness which it offered to man. It may be that Schiller understood this in the moral sense, being a disciple of Kant; but if one looks closer it is clear that in Schiller greatness—and Wallenstein exemplifies this most clearly—can also grow out of the bare nature of man. Even in his youth, Schiller loved what was dangerous and adventurous. This was for him associated with every kind of human greatness, regardless of the direction taken by the human will. To be precise, the striving for moral freedom was to him also an adventure, an adventure which attracted him so strongly because it was dangerous. In his letter to Reinwald he wrote of the Jena philosopher Reinhold: "He will never aspire to daring virtues or wrongdoings, either ideally or actually, and this is bad. I cannot be the friend of any man who has not the faculty for one or the other or both of these".[1]

Nowhere is the inaccuracy and injustice of Nietzsche's angry designation of Schiller as the "Moraltrompeter von Säckingen" more evident than in Schiller's presentation of history. Of course there is the "wisdom" of great men of action in history—for instance, Orange, Gustav Adolf, or Henry IV—but this wisdom must understand how to make the "selfish passions" of other men "the instruments of its fine purposes". For political action, to be successful, requires insight into the wickedness of the world if the plans of the man who acts in history are not to become "a laughing-stock to all the world" and thus remain chimaeras.[2] Certainly Schiller believes that the course of history as a whole, with its inscrutable intimations of "providence" and Nemesis, proceeds in company with the "economy of nature" and with a "higher understanding"; but the progress of reason is being continually menaced by the two reefs: despotism and lawlessness. Therefore this progress requires those natures which are capable of "greatness", which prepare, step by step, even over hazardous, secret, and misleading paths, and through the sacrifice of their own lives, the ultimate moral legislation by freedom. Only thus can man, within the state and within society, proceed towards a last and ultimate realization of his humanity. Only in the solidarity and community of all European peoples can this be achieved. And what Schiller means by

1 *Briefe*, ed. cit., I. p. 399.

2 *SA*, xv. p. 53.

"humanity" is to be found in his treatise 'On the Sublime', where he writes: "All other things obey compulsion; man is the being who exerts will, for force annuls him. Whoever puts force upon us, contends with us for our humanity, no less. Whoever is coward enough to be enforced, throws his humanity away".[1]

[1] *SA*, XII. p. 264. For further discussion, see Benno von Wiese, *Friedrich Schiller*, Stuttgart, 1959, especially the chapters 'Der Geschichtsphilosoph', pp. 330-349, and 'Der Historiker', pp. 350-394.

THE STRUCTURE OF THE PERSONALITY IN SCHILLER'S TRAGIC POETRY

By Ilse Appelbaum Graham

When one thinks of Schiller, one tends to think of an impassioned idealist, fiercely impatient of the constrictions of reality that weighed so heavily upon his life, and enabled, by the undauntedness of his spirit, to transcend them. Whether one turns to the rebellious Elève of the Karlsschule, flinging his in tyrannos in the face of despotic rules and rulers, or recalls the last lines from the dying poet's pen—"O warum bin ich hier geengt, gebunden, beschränkt mit dem unendlichen Gefühl"—the picture of a soaring spirituality remains unchallenged. And what we know of his life, its unending struggle and its unending victory over adversity, confirms it, as do indeed the testimonies of those that knew and loved him.

And yet, this picture is not complete. The idea of young Schiller as a budding preacher fits it well enough—but what about his medical studies? What about his sober realism in matters aesthetic—he liked to call himself a 'Macher'—and his extensive historical studies? What about—to think of an altogether different sphere—his lively interest in rank and recognition, his wide-awake dealings with his publishers, his editorial skill and last, but not least, his appreciation of money? All these betoken an interest in reality and a respect for the things that be which is no less constant, if less conspicuous, than his spirituality.

A little more of that side of Schiller's personality should be known, as a corrective to the dominant side with which we are familiar. It is my wish and hope that this shift of emphasis may make him appear, not indeed less of an idealist: on the contrary, more real in his idealism, more deeply rooted in the reality of human life, for all the loftiness of his vision, than has sometimes been supposed, and therefore more intimately related to us, to our problems and our hopes.

It is indeed a very down to earth young man who in the introduction to his dissertation "Über den Zusammenhang der tierischen Natur des Menschen mit seiner geistigen" calls the stoic ideal "eine schöne Verirrung des Verstandes, ein wirkliches Extremum, das den einen Teil des Menschen allzu enthusiastisch herabwürdigt und uns in den Rang idealischer Wesen erheben will, ohne uns zugleich unserer Menschlichkeit zu entladen;"[1] From the poet of *Die Räuber* the rejection of a view of life simply *because* it is an Extremum may seem unexpected. Here, as indeed throughout the dissertation as a whole, there is a firm grasp of the inalienable totality of the human condition, and this knowledge serves him as a compass to guide him from the first.—And it is a naturalistic thinker with a trained eye on the physiological basis of every mental event who writes, in the *Selbstrecension* of *Die Räuber*: Ich denke . . . überzeugt zu seyn, dass der Zustand des moralischen Übels im Gemüth eines Menschen, ein schlechterdings gewaltsamer Zustand sey, welchen zu erreichen zuförderst das Gleichgewicht der ganzen geistigen Organisation (wenn ich so sagen darf) aufgehoben sein muss, sowie das ganze System der tierischen Haushaltung, Kochung und Scheidung, Puls und Nervenkraft, durcheinander geworfen sein müssen, eh die Natur einem Fieber oder Konvulsion Raum gibt".[2] The human psyche as an organism on the analogy with the biological organism of the human body and subject

1 *Sämmtliche Schriften* ed. Goedeke, Stuttgart. 1867-76. Vol. I, p. 142.

2 Ibid., II, p. 362.

to universal natural laws:— that is a revolutionary conception at which the young poet might well catch his breath: for it never let go of him again. Indeed it proved to be the matrix of his spiritual development, the life thread of his connection with Goethe in his time, and with what is most vital in ours.

Thus it is about this conception of the human psyche as an organic whole that I want to speak to you to-day—about its place in Schiller's dramas, its significance for their thematic and formal structure, and its bearing upon the categories of value commonly connected with Schiller's dramatic poetry.

I think that you will agree that it is a marked feature of Schillerian tragedy that it grows around a nucleus of two central characters, rather than one. Where one thinks of such towering figures as Sophocles' Oedipus, Shakespeare's Lear, Goethe's Iphigenie, one tends, in the case of Schiller's tragedies, to think not so much of single personages but of opposed yet related pairs such as Franz and Karl Moor, Luise and Ferdinand, Posa and Carlos, Wallenstein and Max, Elisabeth and Maria, Isabella and Don Caesar, Don Manuel and Beatrice—(since this tragedy has four principal characters paired in twos). They are all but diametrically opposed, these types: the ones, like Wallenstein, intellectual, ambitious, cautious, fearful to lose their hold over events and to commit themselves, and vacillating until life itself has implemented the choice that they themselves could not bring themselves to make. The others, Karl Moor, Ferdinand and Don Carlos, Maria and Max, Don Caesar and Beatrice, passionate, generous and rash, plunging into commitment and as often as not losing their head in the process, literally as well as metaphorically. And always—rather oddly surely—rising to a sheer sublimity that puts the guarded greatness of their antagonists to shame. They are all but incompatible temperaments, and this fact is reflected in their relationship. It is fraught with tension and an ambiguity that often amounts to open antagonism. Side by side with it are placed the love-entanglements of the antagonists—so often, curiously, with the same person—Karl and Franz love Amalia, Carlos and Posa the Queen, the rival queens love Leicester, the Brothers of Messina Beatrice—; and yet, for all the passion poured into the love relationship, the difficult, refractory relation between the antagonists in the end proves to be the fateful one. As he makes his final choice, the protagonist is turned, not toward the object of his passion, but towards his antagonist. Having renounced Elisabeth in their different ways, Carlos and Posa die for one another. Don Caesar renounces Beatrice in order to obey the stronger call of his murdered brother. Max's despair is wholly oriented to Wallenstein. The issue of Leicester pales before the life and death struggle between the rival queens.—This is surely strange. We do not need to enquire into the nature of the bond between a Romeo and Juliet, or Hero and Leander; even the problematic relation of Hebbel's antagonists are unequivocally based on mutual love; and the bond between Grillparzer's antagonists becomes tragic precisely because it proves to be a spurious attachment on the part of one of them, the younger man. But what is the nature of a bond at once so refractory and so clearly marked off from the realm of passion, and yet so basic? This question deserves a closer enquiry.

But how is such an enquiry to proceed? At once the obvious method suggests itself, of embarking on a direct psychological investigation into character and motives of the tragic antagonists. But have we not many such undertakings, often executed with brilliance and imaginative insight, yet leaving us with a host of contradictory results? The principal reason for such heterogeneity of result is that in focusing our attention on character—the most conspicuous structure in dramatic poetry admittedly —we have forgotten to apprehend this structure as part of the all pervasive structure within which it is organised and of whose stuff it is made: the verbal fabric of the work. The warning words of Valéry come to mind, insisting on the verbal condition of literary characters, ces vivants sans entrailles. I think we shall do well to heed this warning, and to remember this condition at every step of our investigation into their existence and psychology. Accordingly, our enquiry into the relationship between Schiller's antagonists will assume the moderately new look of an enquiry into the connection between the verbal materials of which these figures are composed. What does the connection between the given word clusters which build up the principal characters—their identity or similarity and the identity or similarity of their associations—tell us about the relationship between the antagonists? In answer to this question I should like to examine how Schiller handles certain dominant images associated with his principal characters. There is a tremendous mass of material here and I should really want to present it in full, because it is only by the cumulative force of *all* the evidence pointing in *one* direction that one may hope to carry full conviction in matters such as these. Clearly, such a full presentation cannot be attempted.[1] Limiting myself to some three dramas—representative of the main stages of Schiller's development—I have chosen a very few of the great number of image complexes the poet uses to define the interrelation between the antagonists. Even of these I cannot here give you all the instances. Selected examples must suffice, to indicate something of their configuration and cumulative force.

[1] For a full discussion of these imagistic structures and their function in the aesthetic organisation of Schiller's tragedies, cf. my thesis for the Ph.D. *Schiller's View of Tragedy in the Light of his General Aesthetics*, London, 1951.

One of the most extensive image patterns in Schiller's tragedies is that connected with fire. These images are centred in characters such as Don Carlos, Maria Stuart, Don Caesar, etc. Let me give you some illustrations from the dramas in which they figure. It is not surprising to find images of fire, so commonly associated with the realm of passion, used to articulate Don Carlos' love for Elisabeth. Carlos tells Posa

> Acht höllenbange Monde sind es schon,
> Dass dieses Feur in meinem Busen wütet, (I.2).

and

> Ein entsetzliches Geheimnis brennt auf meiner Brust
> Es soll, es soll heraus. (ibid.).

His heart, he tells the Queen, "fühlt feurig", that she would be happy at his side, (I.5) he reads her letter "entzückt und feurig", (IV.5) and he sums up his final resignation in the words "ein reines Feuer hat mein Wesen geläutert". (V.11) From all sides this semantic pattern is reinforced. Posa describes Carlos' love as a "Fiebertraum", (II.15) and twice calls it "diese hoffnungslose Flamme" (II.15 and IV.21). Alba notes the "heissen Kuss" with which the Prince, at a word from the Queen abruptly ends their quarrel (II.10), and recalls that before her marriage he and she "hatten sich in feurigen Empfindungen verstanden". (III.3). Eboli observes that at the mention of Elisabeth the Prince becomes "lauter Glut". (II.8). Such metaphors may appear merely to reflect rhetorical conventions. Two things, however, speak against this; on the one hand they are firmly centred in the figure of Don Carlos; in respect to him, on the other hand, they are used pervasively, to articulate not only his passion but every phase and facet of his personality. Embedded in such a context, the language of passion is imbued with a richer connotation transcending the merely rhetorical. The religious ardour of the Prince, his political dreams, his relation to Posa, to Eboli, even to his Father, all these, however diverse, are alike articulated in terms of the imagery of fire. We hear of the "Feuerküsse" he bestowed on the cold marble hand of the virgin (II.8); we are told "sein Herz entglüht für eine neue Tugend"; (II.10). "Sein Kopf entbrennt von einer seltsamen Chimäre". (II.10). He is one "dems feurig durch die Wangen lief, wenn man von Freiheit sprach" (I.2). Repeatedly we hear of the "heissen Tränen" he wept for Posa (I.2) and each time the significance of the word is underscored by the stress on Posa's coldness. Different though the relation to his father be, he expresses it in the same terms, saying "ich will Sie feurig lieben" (II.2) and assuring him "wie hoch mein Dank einst flammen wird" (ibid.). Again, his approaches to Eboli are "voll Feuer" (II.8), and withal, the same imagery persists to express his recoil from her advances: "Lassen Sie mich los—Mir wird, als rauchte hinter mir die Welt in Flammen auf". (ibid.)

These limited examples—and they could be multiplied—will indicate something of the consistency and extensiveness with which Schiller uses this image. The actual energy of the pattern, its intensity, is brought about not only by repetition, but by the interaction between different levels of meaning, the literal and factual on the one hand and the metaphorical on the other. The final result of such an interplay is the symbolic, with its characteristic combination of resonance and concreteness.

This interpenetration of the literal and the metaphorical is more obvious in *Die Braut von Messina*. References to fire permeate the text: on the level of the basic scenic données of the play—the drama is acted out in the shadow of Aetna and Beatrice's sanctuary is situated on the slopes of the volcano; on the level of the outer action—the seer puts fire to his hut, also on Aetna's slopes; on the level of reported fact—witness the Father's dream and the two oracles; on the level of direct and indirect characterisation and, most importantly, on the level of the poetic fabric of the play, shot through as it is with metaphors of fire. Assimilated into the poetic organisation on so many levels, the scenic donnée, Aetna, in the end becomes the ultimate poetic symbol of the tragedy. This symbol of an elemental force catastrophically erupting is principally associated with the figures of Beatrice and Don Caesar. She is not only likened to the element—Don Caesar compares her to "Der Sonne Himmelsfeuer"—she *is* the embodied element; on the level of the dream—which discloses the deepest reality, she *is* the flame,

> Die, der Bäume dicht Gezweig
> und das Gebälk ergreifend, prasselnd aufschlug
> und um sich wütend, schnell, das ganze Haus
> In ungeheuer Feuerflut verschlang. (II.5)

To the interpreting consciousness, too, she is the source of the "heisse Liebesglut" that is to redeem the brother's hatred. And if the abode of this elemental being on the slopes of the volcano is symbolic, her escape on which the outer action hinges, is no less so. Twice she breaks forth, to satisfy "Des Herzens heissen Drang" (III.3), driven by "die Macht des Bluts" (II.6); and recalling the words about "den Trieb des Bluts, der mächtig, wie des Feuers veschlossner Gott aus seinen Banden strebte" (IV.1), we realise that her fatal escapades are indeed poetically associated with the eruptions of the fiery element itself. What else does the symbolic action of the old seer betoken? Her release is the release of an elemental force engulfing in destruction all structures of man's devising.

Most closely associated with this imagery is Don Caesar, "der Jüngling mit dem Flammenauge" (II.1). Much imagery of fire is given to him, among others the central image of love arising like a phoenix "aus des Hasses Flammen" and even his knights have a conspicuous share of it. But most important are the choruses which mark his homecoming after the murder of Don Manuel.

Brechet auf, ihr Wunden!
Fliesset, fliesset!
In schwarzen Güssen
Stürzet hervor, ihr Bäche des Bluts.

Stürzet ein, ihr Wände!
Versink, o Schwelle . . .
Schwarze Dämpfe, entsteiget, entsteiget
Qualmend dem Abgrund! (IV.4).

What is this, if not the imagery of the volcano? Don Caesar's nature, like that of Beatrice, is poetically associated with, and formulated through, the imagery of fire erupting with elemental force and destroying all structures of man's devising.[1]

And lastly, Maria Stuart, whose destiny Schiller defined as "heftige Passionen zu erfahren und zu entzünden": imagery of fire converges from all sides to articulate her inflammatory nature. She herself speaks of "meiner Leiden brennendes Gefühl" (III.4) and likens her being to the fiery element. Friend and enemy concur in this characterisation, in the most varied contexts, whether we hear Kennedy recount the feminine follies of her youth, or Burleigh describe her political schemes, or Paulet her machinations from her very prison cell, or whether we see Mortimer respond to her incensed mood—it is always in the same terms—in terms of an uncontrollable conflagration. Kennedy calls Maria's passion for Bothwell "der Wahnsinn blinder Liebesglut" (I.4).

1 Cf. my article *Element into Ornament; the Alchemy of Art. A Reading of Schiller's Die Braut von Messina* (in press) which deals fully with the imagery of fire and its bearing upon the figure of Beatrice.

He is "der Schreckliche, der Euch erhitzte" (ibid.). Maria's very cheeks "Glühten nur vom Feuer des Verlangens (ibid.).

Burleigh calls her

> Die Ate dieses ewgen Kriegs, die mit
> der Liebesfackel dieses Reich entzündet (II.3)

and mocks at the integrity of her aspirations

> Da Ihr das Reich entzünden, durch die Flammen
> Des Bürgerkriegs zum Throne steigen wolltet. (I.17).

Paulet invokes the same imagery.

> Doch wusste sie aus diesen engen Banden
> Den Arm zu strecken in die Welt, die Fackel
> Des Bürgerkrieges in das Reich zu schleudern (I.1).

And finally, Mortimer's adoption of the imagery associated with Maria to express his passionate response to her—he looks at her "mit glühenden Blicken", speaks of "glühende Eisenzangen," addresses her as "Heissgeliebte" as "des Lebens wärmste Brust", etc., etc. (all III.6)—serves palpably to confirm the trend of action and imagery alike: Maria's being is an elemental force that cannot be arrested or contained.

Placed in such a powerful context, even the stage-direction preceding her final affront to Elisabeth deserves to be taken, not merely as an aid to the actress, but as a vital contribution to the thematic texture of the play. Maria addresses her rival "Vor Zorn glühend". At the climactic moment of the tragedy, when Maria strikes the mortal blow at her enemy and thereby seals her own doom, when she sums up the truth about her own being, she stands suffused with the glow of inner fire: she is all fire. We know it, and Elisabeth confirms it later, when she recalls Maria's look: "Als sollte mich der Blick zu Boden blitzen." (IV.10). What better image of unalloyed flame is there than that of lightening?

And what is the truth that Maria holds up to her enemy?

> Weh Euch, wenn sie von Euren Taten einst
> Den Ehrenmantel zieht, womit Ihr gleissend
> Die wilde Glut verstohlner Lüste deckt. (III.4)

There is fire in Elisabeth too. But it is unsanctioned and concealed from the eyes of the world. Elisabeth knows that this is the truth about her. She kills Maria because Maria has revealed the stain in her being and thus invalidated her claim—the crucial lines in the great monologue which lead up to her decision significantly take up the image of the covering cloak and the compromising secret it hides which Maria has used.

This then is the relation of two antagonists, expressed in terms of the imagery of fire: the one, Maria, is consistently associated with an open and spreading conflagration, enveloping all her being. The other contains a fire, secretly, covertly, and alluded to, significantly, in one albeit climactic reference.[1]

And what about the other tragic protagonists, Marquis Posa on the one hand and Isabella and Don Manuel on the other? In what is probably the most "hotly" debated speech in the drama the Marquis begs the King not to fear him. These are his words.

> Die lächerliche Wut
> Der Neuerung . . .
> Wird mein Blut nie erhitzen . . .
> Kann ein Gemälde Ihre Ruhe trüben?—
> Ihr Atem löscht es aus. (III.10)

A most ambiguous statement, this; in the very act of denying the passionate spark in him he affirms it. For

1 And this difference is pointed not only by the use of qualitatively different imagery, but by quantitative means. Against the overwhelming number of images that converge upon Maria there is *one*—albeit an absolutely climactic one in virtue of its placing and its implications, that illuminates the secret presence of the element in Elisabeth.

does he not partake of it through the image he uses, and the associations it evokes? And what about the image in which he sums up his self-contained innocuousness? The image of himself as a work of art? There can be no doubt that through the word "auslöschen" this passage is brought within the orbit of the imagery of fire. Posa tells us that a work of art, too, may burn with the fire of inspiration; but it is a fire which is composed into form and contained within its bounds. This interpretation may seem to read more into Posa's words than they will bear. That this is not so, becomes clear from the King's response to Posa's declaration of faith: The King can tolerate Posa

Um dieser Enthaltung willen, solche Meinungen,
Mit solchem Feuer doch umfasst, verschwiegen
Zu haben bis auf diesen Tag—um dieser
Bescheidenen Klugheit willen . . . (III.10).

In the light of this metaphor—so important because it motivates the King's leniency and thus encourages Posa to assume his fatal double rôle—the earlier apparently wayward allusion to fire turns out to be a perfectly controlled, if submerged, image. Associations which were scarcely perceptible in Posa's own words, are now explicit. The denial of the inner fire in words like "Enthaltung" and "bescheiden", the tortuous syntactical structure, the anxious stress on control and the grudging admission of passionate impulses—all this confirms the association of Posa (and for that matter, of the King) with imagery of fire carefully guarded and concealed, just as conversely Carlos was found to be associated with images of open conflagration.

And even the association of the "Gemälde" with the imagery of fire was not as arbitrary as may have seemed. Towards the end of the drama both images reappear, this time fully and explicitly integrated in words rich with symbolic meaning:

Was geht es König Phillip an, wenn seine
"Verklärung" in Escurial den Maler,
Der vor ihr steht, mit Ewigkeit entzündet? (IV.21)

Posa asks Elisabeth as he prepares to die for his friend and their ideals. He has learnt to see himself, not as a work of art, but as a living human being, related to beauty, to be sure, but responding to it with a passion which fires action, and leads out into life.

In *Die Braut von Messina*, as opposed to the earlier dramas, a great deal of the imagery associated with fire has been given over to the tragic protagonists, to Isabella and Don Manuel, a measure of the poet's increasing preoccupation with verbal structures and his subordination to them of character. For the imagery itself connected with these figures evinces the same telling twist as in the earlier dramas: it is imagery of suppression. Isabella likens her son's hatred to "des Feuers *eingepresste* Glut". (I.1) Again:

Des *unterirdschen* Feuers schreckliche
Geburt ist alles, eine Lavarinde
Liegt *aufgeschichtet* über dem Gesunden (I.4).

And again:

Nichts Kleines war es, solche Heimlichkeit
Verhüllt zu tragen diese langen Jahre
. . . und ins Herz *zurückzudrängen*
Den Trieb des Bluts, der mächtig, wie des Feuers
Verschlossner Gott, aus seinen Banden strebte! (IV.1).

With this imagery the figure of Manuel is associated through his dominant character trait of "Verschlossenheit" which is testified to by the chorus (I.7 and I.8), by Don Caesar,

Nicht *meine* Weise ist's, geheimnisvoll
Mich zu verhüllen, Mutter. Frei und offen
Wie meine Stirne trag ich mein Gemüt; (II.5)

by Isabella,

> Des Vater eignen Sinn und Geist erkenn ich
> In meinem erstgebornen Sohn. *Der* liebte
> Von jeher, sich verborgen in sich selbst
> Zu spinnen und den Ratschluss zu bewahren
> Im unzugangbar fest verschlossenen Gemüt. (II.5)

and finally, by Don Manuel himself who confesses his reticence to the chorus in an elaborate metaphor preceding his disclosure and confirms it by his behaviour.

> Geflügelt ist das Glück und schwer zu binden,
> Und in verschlossner Lade wirds bewahrt,
> Das Schweigen ist zum Hüter ihm gesetzt,
> Und rasch entfliegt es, wenn Geschwätzigkeit
> Voreilig wagt, die Decke zu erheben. (I.7)

Words like "verschlossen, bewahren, verborgen, Decke", and the atmosphere of fearful superstition they create form so many links associating Don Manuel with the imagery of locked-up elemental forces.

Thus the tragic protagonists are all associated with images of fire which is secret and contained, just as their antagonists are consistently associated with images of open and uncontrolled conflagration. This interlocking of the image materials associated with the principal figures suggests the existence of a close interconnection between them; and indeed, we have not yet done justice to the intricate precision with which the image-complexes associated with the antagonists do in fact interlock. We said that the tragic protagonists suppress the fire that is a part of their being, deep inside them, there to keep it imprisoned. This inner constriction, so the imagery tells us, in the case of their antagonists becomes a palpable dramatic reality! They *are* imprisoned, in fact as well as metaphorically, and vigilantly guarded by their captors. And here it is important to remember that in Schiller's hands external données such as being arrested or imprisoned are so closely interwoven with the poetic fabric of his plays that they become invested with symbolic force.

Don Carlos describes himself as a

> Gefangener
> Auf diesem Grund, wo ich einst Herr sein werde (II.2).

And although his words at this point refer to his father, their reference soon broadens and deepens: for it is Posa who obtains the warrant for his friend's arrest and uses it, an action which links him to Alba's sinister policy of keeping "einen Vorrat Blutsentenzen", and in a less concrete sense it is Posa "Der Sohn und Vater zu Gefangenen macht". (IV.22). Indeed, it is in prison that the final encounter between him and Carlos is staged.

The sanctuary in which Isabella is keeping Beatrice, in the course of the drama comes to stand for something of a prison: "Verborgener war sie nicht im Schoss der Erde" (II.6), we hear, and Beatrice herself is called "die Wohlverschlossene". And if she says of her elopement with Manuel

> Die Pforten durchbrach ich der heiligen Zelle,

and of her surrender to him

> Eindringt der Gott auch zu verschlossnen Toren,
> Zu Perseus Turm hat er den Weg gefunden. (II.1)

the suggestion of imprisonment is underscored by the associated movement of breaking in or out. Don Manuel is closely connected with this image pattern not only because he guards over Beatrice's every movement, "ernst und finster", nor indeed only because of many direct references to her secret place of confinement, but, most importantly, because of his persistent poetic association with images of imprisoning and locking up.

The apostrophe to the "Geflügelte Glück"

—Und in verschlossner Lade wirds bewahrt,
Das Schweigen ist zum Hüter ihm gesetzt—

on a deeper poetic level are words about Beatrice, so often apostrophied as "Das Glück" in this play, and reveal his superstitious preoccupation with keeping her in safe captivity.

Maria Stuart's imprisonment at the hands of Elisabeth is of course the principal dramatic donnée of the tragedy and as such needs no elaboration. The references to her prison are legion, and there is not one that is not characterised by a marked emotional timbre. Those by herself and her friends stress the cruelty of her physical constriction—Mortimer speaks of "des Kerkers Schmach" (I.6), Maria of "die Gefängnisnacht" (I.6), the "traurige Gruft" (III.I), Shrewsbury of "ihres Kerkers Gräbernacht" (II.4), whilst Kennedy calls her "lebendig eingemauert" (I.I); as against this, the references of her opponents are marked by superstitious fear lest no constriction will suffice to hold her. I shall quote one from many.

Kein Eisengitter schützt vor ihrer List.
Weiss ich, ob diese Stäbe nicht durchfeilt,
Nicht dieses Zimmers Boden, diese Wände,
Von aussen fest, nicht hohl von innen sind,
Und den Verrat einlassen, wenn ich schlafe?
Vom Schlummer jagt die Furcht mich auf, ich gehe
Nachts um, wie ein gequälter Geist, erprobe des
Schlosses Riegel und der Wächter Treu
Und sehe zitternd jeden Morgen kommen (I.I).

It will readily be seen that from the start the references to Maria's prison are not handled factually, but emotively and imaginatively. The tremendous emphasis upon the physical paraphernalia of imprisonment, the stress by her friends on its indignity and by her foes on its ineffectuality, serves to create a growing sense that it is an event of an altogether different order which is symbolically enacted within symbolic prison walls: the constriction and eventual release of a force which no prison bars can contain.

This symbolic import is developed throughout the drama and emerges in full force at the end, in a significant modulation of the prison image used by Paulet, when Maria says to Melvil:

> Wie ein Unsterblicher auf goldnen Wolken
> Herniederfährt, wie den Apostel einst
> Der Engel führte aus des Kerkers Banden,
> Ihn hält kein Riegel, keines Hüters Schwert,
> Er schreitet mächtig durch verschlossne Pforten,
> Und im Gefängnis steht er glänzend da,
> So überrascht mich hier der Himmelsbote (v.7).

And it is significant to see that Shrewsbury asks Maria's keeper, Elisabeth, to descend to Maria's prison in imagistic terms that closely anticipate the ones used in this final formulation. By such means and others—Leicester, the first Lord of the Realm, reveals that he too is in fact the Queen's prisoner—Elisabeth comes to be associated with this verbal pattern in its deeper symbolic as well as its literal significance.

There is yet one other aspect of the image material we have been discussing, to which I should like to draw your attention: this might be called its topographical aspect. Schiller visualises the act of suppression of part of ourselves—the elemental part which is symbolised by fire—in terms of a spatial image. Whether Isabella likens her son's hatred to "des unterirdschen Feuers schreckliche Geburt" (I.4), or whether, in an analogous context, Rudenz says in *Wilhelm Tell*

> Mein überschwellend und empörtes Herz
> Hab ich hinabgedrückt in meinen Busen (III.3)

the suppressed elemental impulses are consistently envisaged as being pushed down into the depth of the psyche. Is it not significant that the prison existence of the tragic antagonists, too, is envisaged as a life lived in a subterranean region? This imagistic conception prevails no matter what the historical or geographical facts. We have no evidence that the historical Maria lived a subterranean life during her imprisonment at Fotheringhay, yet constant reference is made to the "Gefängnisnacht", "Des Kerkers Gräbernacht" "die traurige Gruft".[1] The general poetic image that crystallises from such instances is that Maria in fact lives in a realm below that in which Elisabeth resides. This spatial image underlies Leicester's vision of the future:

> Stehst du nicht blühend da in Jugendkraft?
> Welkt jene nicht mit jedem Tag zum Grabe?
> Bei Gott! Du wirst, ich hoffs, noch viele Jahre
> Auf ihrem Grabe wandeln, ohne dass
> Du selber sie hinabzustürzen brauchtest—(II.2).

In the light of such passages even the staging of Maria's death—her execution takes place "im unteren Saale", beneath the feet of the terrified Leicester—surely signifies a good deal more than Schiller's taste for the horrific.

The same may be said of Beatrice's sanctuary, of which we hear, in a strictly expositional piece of information that it lies

> Hinterm Waldgebirge, das zum Aetna
> Sich langsam *steigend* hebt . . . (II.6).

Yet images crowd in thick and fast suggesting that Beatrice's abode is in the bowels of the earth. "Verborgner war sie nicht im Schoss der Erde", we are told,

1 Maria asks "bin ich dem finstern Gefängnis entstiegen?" (III.1). She desribes Elisabeth as the one "die mich in diese Schmach hinunterstiess" (III.4); Talbot asks here: "steige in ihres Kerkers Gräbernacht hinab" (II.4), Mortimer says "Euch kann kein Kerker tief genug begraben" (I.6), etc.

and the image persists when Beatrice herself is described as "Die Tiefverborgene", and her refuge as "des Lebens Grab", etc. Such subtle distortions of the outer scene testify to the poet's preoccupation with the inner topography of the human mind and its intimate connection with outer circumstance. The spatial imagery associated with the phenomenon of inner suppression is projected outward and is faithfully reflected there in the presentation of the antagonist's external plight.

This then is the configuration of the images that go into the making of the principal figures and of the relation between them. On the one hand we see an elemental drive suppressed within the protagonist; on the other we see the same drive embodied in his antagonist. And as the protagonist imprisons the elemental force deep within himself, so also does he imprison the person of his antagonist, body and spirit. There are a great many more image patterns used by the poet to build up the principal figures and they all complement one another in an analogous fashion. In view of such evidence we must conclude that the poet has embodied one aspect of his protagonist in the separate being of his opponent—a procedure which in keeping with modern critical usage I propose to call Externalisation. To say this is to suggest an unusually close interconnection between the antagonists. But of what nature precisely is this connection? Is it a relation of similarity or of partial identity? Here again the imagery may provide the answer.

Maria accuses her rival of smothering her deeper life within her: "Die wilde Glut verstohlner Lüste". In the same breath almost she says of herself:

> Ich bin nur noch der Schatten der Maria. (III.4).

Isabella's vital impulses smoulder in the depth of her soul, all but stifled; Beatrice the while leads a life that is a living death, in a refuge that is "des Lebens Grab" (I.7).

> Und so erwuchs ich still am stillen Orte
> In Lebens Glut den Schatten beigesellt (II.11).

When Carlos says

> Auch mir hat einst von einem Karl geträumt,
> Dems feurig durch die Wangen lief, wenn man
> Von Freiheit sprach—doch der ist lang begraben. (I.2)

he is relating his plight to his unhappy love. The images he uses, however, point in another direction. Anticipating as they do Posa's words to the King:

> Meine Wünsche verwesen hier.
> Die lächerliche Wut
> Der Neuerung . . .
> Wird mein Blut nie erhitzen (III.10)

they poetically link Carlos' predicament with his friend's endeavour to suppress his deeper life. Whilst Posa denies his passions, Carlos' life is at an ebb. When he accepts them, life returns to the Prince. To witness the change that comes over him, as gazing at his new found friend he cold-shoulders Alba, is to witness a spiritual blood transfusion (V.1 and V.2). Such intimate connections suggest something more than a relationship—however close—between separate personalities. They irresistibly suggest an actual dependence, an interlacing of life-threads. Moreover, this dependence appears to be reciprocal.

Exhausted and distorted but a little while before—

> Alle ihre Züge
> Wie eines Sterbenden entstellt—(IV.21)

the Queen observes—Posa is presently suffused with the very life that he himself has kindled in the Prince:

> Welch plötzliche
> Veränderung in deinen Zügen?

Carlos marvels—

So hab ich dich nie gesehen. Stolzer hebt sich
Deine Brust und deine Blicke leuchten. (v.3)[1]

This mutual dependence is illuminated by Shrewsbury's words:

Ich habe Deinen edlern Teil
Nicht retten können, (v.15)

he says after Maria's death, and it is to Elisabeth that his words are addressed. In murdering Maria, she has murdered a part of herself. Both Queens know that they share one destiny. Maria, when she warns her "sister": "Ehrt in mir Euch selbst" and Elisabeth when on hearing the news of Maria's death she exclaims:

Das Grab deckt *meine* Furcht. (v.12).

In *Die Braut von Messina*, this interdependence of the antagonists is most unequivocally formulated as deriving from an ultimate one-ness. Oneness is writ large over the tragedy, quite literally; articulated in a great variety of ways, oneness is simply and persistently imprinted on our consciousness by the steady italicised use, throughout the tragedy, of the numeral *ein* and its antithetical *zwei*. When Isabella exclaims, near the beginning of the drama

Vergessen ganz musst ich den *einen* Sohn,
Wenn ich der Nähe mich des andern freute,
O meine Mutterliebe ist nur ewig eine
Und meine Söhne waren ewig zwei—(I.4).

She seems to envisage the possibility of a oneness which does in a real sense transcend the empirical fact of two-foldness and division. Such an idea underlies her simile of the Theban brothers, a pair so closely intertwined that murder and suicide fuse in one indivisible act.

Leib gegen Leib, wie das thebanische Paar,
Rückt aufeinander an, und, wutvoll ringend,

1 Compare this description with Posa's earlier avowal—Meine Wünsche/verwesen hier (die Hand auf die Brust gelegt) and Die lächerliche Wut/der Neuerung/wird mein Blut nie erhitzen . . . (III.10).

Umfanget euch in eherner Umarmung.
Leben um Leben tauschend siege jeder,
Den Dolch einbohrend in des andern Brust. (I.5).

The same conception of oneness is formulated in Don Manuels' "... Wir sind jetzt *ein* Haupt und *ein* Gemüt". (III.2) This imagistic conception is borne out by the action. Don Manuel's murder does mean Don Caesar's suicide. For Don Caesar too, recognises that, "in *einem* Fall verstrickt", a separate life is unfeasible. He retrospectively confirms the oneness of their lives through the oneness of their death; asking that their ashes be buried in *einem* Aschenkruge, that

Ein Totenmal den Mörder
Zugleich mit dem Gemordeten umschliesst,
Ein Stein sich wölbet über beider Staube. (IV.6).

This indivisible unity of the antagonists has found its most revealing formulation in the imagistic conception of the members of one family as members, or organs, of one organism. Don Caesar likens the bond between himself and Beatrice to the indissoluble bond between the parts of one organism when he says,

Der Geist verlasse
Eher die Glieder, eh ich von dir scheide (II.2).

Beatrice takes up this image, on realising that she is being drawn into the vortex

Dieses furchtbaren Geschlechts,
Das sich selbst vertilgend hasst,
Gegen seine eignen Glieder
Wütend mit Erbittrung rast. (II.3).

And Manuel, too, confirms a corresponding sense in the words

... Wir sind jetzt *ein* Haupt und *ein* Gemüt. (III.2).

Such organic images recur throughout this tragedy, as indeed they do throughout Schiller's dramatic work from *Die Räuber* onwards to *Wilhelm Tell.* They confirm what the interlocking image patterns have increasingly suggested: the relation between the antagonists is not that between two similarly constituted but separate entities. It is in fact the relation between constituent parts that together share one common life and constitute one organic whole. This awareness of a complementary relation between the antagonists is created, principally, by the extensive use of synecdoche. Through the consistent identification of the protagonist with organic structures like "Haupt" and "Auge"—symbols of our rational functions—and the corresponding identification of his antagonist with "Herz" and "Gemüt"—symbols of the passional functions of feeling, sensation and instinctual drives which Schiller includes under the "sinnliche Triebe"—we come to regard each figure as the living embodiment of the functions denoted by the associated symbol, and we are kept reminded of the fact that only together do they form a viable organic whole.

"An organism," so the Concise Oxford Dictionary tells us "—is an organised body with connected interdependent parts sharing a common life". This definition fits the facts and findings from the tragedies perfectly. As the parts of a biological organism are mutually indispensable, so are the partners in the relationship which is the crucible of Schiller's dramatic structures. For each embodies a function which is vital to the whole of which they are part, and thus to the other; and neither can hope to flourish in isolation. Each partner realises his own potential as he honours the life of the other, helping it to realise itself. We have seen such a flowering in Posa's personality when at long last he gives his due to his friend; too late, it is true, to save their lives, but not too late to restore him to inner wholeness and a new vitality. The same is true of Wallenstein and Johanna, of Maria and Don Caesar, and from all sides we could quote words expressing the incredulous sense of enrichment and regeneration they experience as, honouring the other, they at last honour "the other" in themselves, thus regaining a wholeness of spirit they had lost.

Conversely, the arrogation by one organic part of the vitality that by rights belongs to the other, leads not only to the other's destruction, but to the disintegration of the whole that sustains them both, and thus, eventually, to the destruction of the usurping function. This law of organic nature holds with equal force in the world of Schiller's tragedy. The destruction of Karl Moor, of Fiesco's Leonore, of Don Carlos and Posa, of Maria Stuart, of Romanov means the spiritual degeneration and atrophy of Franz, of Fiesco, of Don Philip, of Elisabeth, of Demetrius, to mention only some. And is it not revealing that in every one of these figures Schiller has resorted to the outward symbol of the Usurper? For Usurpers they all are, arrogating to themselves the life that belongs to the corpus commune; and their psychic deterioration is reflected, not only in the destruction of their antagonist, but more palpably in their political drift from freedom to despotism, and from despotism—wherever historical considerations permitted such a conclusion—to death.[1]

Schiller has shown on yet another level the operation of the organic law whereby the usurping part of an

1 Franz Moor seeks to usurp the life and estate of his elder brother and his father; Fiesco usurps the freedom of the Republic and sets himself up as Genoas new tyrant—"Ein Augenblick Fürst hat das Mark des ganzen Daseins verschlungen—" (III.2). Philip has not only ousted the old emperor at the beginning of his career: at its close he also robs his son of his Queen and his throne. Elisabeth by force usurps the place of Maria, true and legitimate claimant of the throne; the ruling family of Messina are conquerors who have forced their rule on the people of Messina; and Demetrius, finally, turns out to be no less of a false pretender than Boris from whom he wrested the Russian Crown.—Thus in all these tragedies—and in those that I have not explicitly mentioned here—the poetic symbol of the usurper has a threefold significance. It articulates an inner psychological process within the principal character—the arrogation by one function of the vitality that belongs to the whole—and it reflects this inner process in the usurpation of the life of the antagonist and—at one remove—of the body politic as a whole.

organism deteriorates and eventually destroys itself. As we have seen, each antagonist embodies as his dominant tendency that function which in the other is neglected. By this distribution each, although heavily overbalanced on one side, still contains the potential of the other side that is embodied in his opponent: in this potential wholeness, in fact, lies his claim to humanity. In a whole series of secondary characters Schiller has externalised one function of the antagonists once again, this time in complete isolation. Such figures are Mortimer and Leicester, extensions as it were of Maria's sensuality and Elisabeth's vacillating ambition; Spiegelberg, extension of Franz Moor's megalomaniac fancies; Gräfin Terzky, and, at one remove, Butler, extensions of Wallenstein's will to power. Again, Talbot and Queen Isabeau are extensions of the warring factions within Johanna— her rational and her instinctual drives; whilst Rudenz and Melchthal, themselves embodiments of the two sides of Tell's make-up, are once again reflected in the extremes of Parricida and Ruodi, the fisherman. Such extensions do not merely magnify the functions they embody: they also distort them. In some degree all these figures are carricatures of the principal characters they reflect, and necessarily so, because the one-sided development of one function at the cost of the rest inevitably leads to its degeneration. The warring functions *within* Johanna are distorted in the pure intellectuality of Talbot on the one hand and the unrestricted instinctuality of Queen Isabeau on the other. The psychic elements that combine in Tell, already imperfectly mirrored in the one-sidedness of Rudenz and Melchthal, are hardly recognisable in the extremeness of Parricida and Ruodi. Wallenstein's will to power assumes more than life-size proportions in Gräfin Terzky; in Butler it becomes an altogether inhuman thing. The reason in each case is that, while the single function is contained within the living context of the organism, it is modified by its interaction with the rest of the functions and faithfully reflects the life quality of the whole. Disengaged from this organic bond, it inevitably becomes anarchic; a development which is expressed in the obdurate narrowness and ultimate self-destructiveness of the figure in which it is embodied.

Thus we may discern two organising principles operating throughout Schiller's tragedies and determining their inner form: the one is the conception of the human psyche as an organic whole—a principle making for unity and cohesion; the other is the externalisation—or dramatisation—of a single aspect of that psyche in a separate being, a principle making for disjunction. The polarity of these two principles results in the characteristically dynamic structure of personality and interpersonal relationship which is, I think, the outstanding feature of Schillerian tragedy. A basic duality, or, to use a formulation from the *Ästhetische Briefe*—a basic "Antagonism der Kräfte", is built into the very heart of these tragedies. Yet no less basic is the untenableness of such a condition—the pull towards unity. For each of the partners is conceived as a part, radically insufficient in himself. Just as in the tragic protagonist the passional functions symbolised by fire are neglected and repressed, so, conversely, the rational functions which are dominant in him, in the antagonist are all but undeveloped. And just as the antagonist embodies in a separate being the neglected passional drives of the tragic hero, so the latter, in his being, embodies those rational functions which are repressed in the antagonist.[1] Thus each of the

[1] This aspect of the relationship between the antagonists is poetically articulated through the consistent use of visual imagery. The intellectual drives predominantly associated with the tragic protagonist are symbolised in the intensity and range of his perception. Their paucity in the tragic antagonist—who is propelled by passion—is as consistently symbolised by his blindness, i.e., the negation of vision: a procedure that is analogous to the poetic characterisation of the protagonist by the imagery of stifled fire.

tragic antagonists is basically incomplete, unable to live except through his opponent. Only together do they achieve personhood.

So radical is their insufficiency, and so compelling the pull towards integration inherent in their poetic configuration, that we are led to complete this movement in a creative albeit controlled act of the imagination. We are led to conceive the scheme of the ideal person behind the real persons, the psychic organism in which they are designed to inhere and whose life they are destined to share.

Critics have often said, in different formulations, that Schiller's tragedy depicts "den Leidensweg der Idee in dieser Welt". I think that there is some truth in this perception of an Idea as the real hero of Schiller's tragedy: only it is not the idea of the "Übersinnliche", but rather the idea of regenerated aesthetic humanity which is in truth a spiritual organism, that is the invisible tragic hero of Schiller's poetry, glimpsed from afar and invoked time and again, only to be destroyed.

This ideal has become realised in *Wilhelm Tell*, the drama in which Schiller transcends tragedy. Here, the quest for organic wholeness which is at the heart of the tragedies is relegated to the circumference, to the strife and eventual union of Rudenz and Melchthal and the estates they represent. The functions they embody in isolation have become fully integrated in the figure of Tell. He is the ideal person of the tragedies become flesh and blood, the first and only person in the full sense of the word that Schiller created. And to say this is tantamount to saying that Tell is in truth what Schiller's tragic protagonists aim at being, yet fail to be: an aesthetic personality. Here, for the first time, is an independent being standing by himself and relying on his own resources, token of the fact that he is a self-sufficient psychic organism with all his functions intact and all his potential freed, sustained by the life of the whole and sustaining it in turn.

It will be recalled that this conception of the human psyche as an organism on the analogy of a biological organism pre-occupied Schiller from the outset of his intellectual career. It recurs with unbroken continuity throughout his theoretical writings. In his dissertation *Über den Zusammenhang der thierischen Natur des Menschen mit seiner geistigen* he speaks of the "Organismus des geistigen Lebens"[1] and this formulation is not to be taken metaphorically but quite literally: for his whole thesis of the interdependence of body and soul rests on the assumption of their structural identity. The same conception pervades *Über das gegenwärtige Teutsche Theater*, with its persistent medical and pharmaceutical imagery to describe the psychological effect of passions presented on the stage.[2] In the *Selbstrezension* of *Die Räuber*, Schiller describes the moral decay of Franz as a disruption of the balance "der ganzen geistigen Organisation"[3]. Again, the analogy between the physical and psychic organism underlies many a formulation in *Die Schaubühne als moralische Anstalt betrachtet* e.g., a statement such as this on the effect of art: " . . . heilsame Leidenschaften erschüttern unsere schlummernde Natur und treiben das Blut in frischen Wallungen"[4]. The same conception becomes explicit in the introduction to the *Philosophische Briefe* where we read: "Scepticismus und Freidenkerei sind die Fieberparoxysmen des menschlichen Geistes, und müssen durch eben die unnatürliche Erschütterung die sie in *gut organisierten Seelen* verursachen, zuletzt die

1 *Sämmtliche Schriften*, ed. cit., I, p. 144.

2 Ibid., II, pp. 80, 81, 84 cf. also p. 85 where the notion developed in the dissertation of body and soul as two identically structured instruments is echoed.

3 Ibid., p. 362.

4 Ibid., III. p. 524.

Gesundheit befestigen helfen"[1]. In *Der Geisterseher* we read: "das moralische Wesen ist also in sich selbst vollendet und beschlossen wie das, welches wir das organische nennen, beschlossen durch seine Moralität, wie dieses durch seinen Bau, und diese Moralität ist eine Beziehung, die von dem was ausser ihm vorgeht, durchaus unabhängig ist"[2]. The conception of the human psyche as an organism emerges as the central thought of the *Ästhetische Briefe*, in the 7th letter, where Schiller draws a detailed analogy between the evolution of the human psyche towards higher forms of organisation and the evolution of more differentiated physical organisms from primitive beginnings.[3] It finally emerges as the crowning conception of the essay in the formulation of the "Wechselwirkung" between the rational and the passional drives of the personality which are related in such a manner that each realises the peak of its own potential precisely through the activity of the other, such that "die Wirksamkeit des einen die Wirksamkeit des andern zugleich begründet und begrenzt, und wo jeder einzelne für sich gerade dadurch zu seiner höchsten Verkündigung gelangt, dass der andere tätig ist."[4].

It is, however, in the earlier essay, in the *Philosophische Gespräch* of *Der Geisterseher*, that Schiller defines the moral implications of his conception of the human psyche most unequivocally: "Moralität"—he writes—"ist eine

1 Ibid., IV. p. 32.

2 Ibid., IV. p. 306. The organic conception developed here, and in particular the notion of an inner purposiveness, closely anticipates Kant's definitions in *Die Kritik der Urteilskraft*. It is the precise biological connotation of Schiller's concept—a feature that predates his acquaintance with Kant—which is the hallmark of his thinking from the beginning and distinguishes it sharply from Herder's handling of the concept.—For a closer discussion of Schiller's concept of the organism, cf. my thesis, op. cit., pp. 298 ff.

3 ibid., X. p. 295 cf. also the analogy in letter six, where the harmonious development of the psyche is compared with the beauty of the body brought about "durch das freye und gleichförmige Spiel der Glieder". (ibid., X. p. 294).

4 Ibid., X. p. 320.

Beziehung, die nur innerhalb der Seele, ausserhalb ihr nie gedacht werden kann". And he continues: "Sobald wir uns also eine Handlung als in der Seele vorhanden denken, gehört sie einem eigenen Ganzen zu, das seinen Mittelpunkt in sich selbst hat, aus welchem alles fliesst, was es giebt, gegen welchen alles strömt, was es empfängt. Dieser Mittelpunkt ist . . . nichts anderes als der innewohnende Trieb, alle seine Kräfte zum Wirken zu bringen, oder was ebensoviel sagt, zur höchsten Kundmachung seiner Existenz zu gelangen. In diesen Zustand setzen wir die Vollkommenheit des moralischen Wesens, so . . . wie wir ein musikalisches Instrument vollkommen nennen, wenn alle Theile desselben an seiner Wirkung den höchsten Antheil nehmen, dessen sie fähig sind und um dessentwillen sie vereinigt sind. Das Verhältnis nun, in welchem die Tätigkeiten des moralischen Wesens zu diesem Principium stehen, bezeichnen wir mit dem Namen der *Moralität;* und eine Handlung ist moralisch gut oder böse, je nach dem sie sich jenem nähert oder von ihm entfernt, es fördert oder hindert. Eine gute Handlung" is one "wobei mehr Kräfte thätig waren und umgekehrt". "Und dadurch, dass weniger Kräfte bei ihr thätig waren, wird eine schlimme Handlung schlimm, and so umgekehrt".[1]

You will readily grant the organic connotation of this remarkable passage with its central image of a pulsating heart—"ein eigenes Ganzes, das seinen Mittelpunkt in sich selbst hat, aus welchem alles fliesst, was es giebt, gegen welchen alles strömt, was es empfängt". You will also agree that the criterion of moral value developed here is entailed in the conception of the human psyche as an organic whole. Here, as there, the only absolute value is the self realisation of the whole, its optimal life-performance. On this absolute value every other value is contingent.

1 Ibid., IV. pp. 300-302.

To draw an absolute distinction between one set of psychic functions and the other on the ground that one is inherently more valuable than the other, is as meaningless as to judge the brain to be more valuable than the heart. Both are valuable by virtue of the differentiated function they perform, and their value is determined by their contribution to the common life.

In the face of such valuations, can we continue to apply to Schiller Kant's metaphysical scheme of the "Sinnliche" versus the "Übersinnliche" with the fixed scale of values this implies? Schiller scholarship has tacitly assumed that such a basic dichotomy exists and that the rational functions of the human psyche and the values accessible to them are intrinsically more valuable than the passional functions and the values they realise. Such a scheme becomes untenable in the face of Schiller's dynamic and functional view of the human psyche conceived as an organic whole. Equally inapplicable is Kant's Absolute of the Pure Will which carries over into the moral field the primacy of the rational function and of the universal values germane to it. This absolute has been widely held to be operative throughout Schiller's tragedies. Yet its oustanding characteristic lies in the fact that it makes no reference to the condition of the empirical part of our nature, to our sense being. Unconditional moral value is attached to the will that is determined by reason alone, in deliberate disregard of the dictates of sense and feeling. But Schiller's concern is with the psyche as an organic whole. From this naturalistic premiss it is strictly meaningless to isolate any part, however differentiated, from the living whole within which it functions, and to put an absolute premium on it.

This, indeed, is the poetic judgement made by Schiller's tragedies in their entirety, and made most forcefully by their formal structure. The symmetrical juxtaposition of the antagonists and the analogous arrangement of the secondary characters reflecting them tells us that the excess of the rational functions in one group is no better than the excess of sense and feeling in the other. No matter which function usurps the rest, it is equally at fault by reason of usurping the life of the whole instead of serving it. Posa's "Egoism der Vernunft" is as much of an aberration as Carlos' "Egoism der Sinne"; Elisabeth's overweening rationality as immoral as Maria's sensuality; Rudenz' spiritual presumption as inadequate as Melchthal's blind instinctuality. Even Johanna is thus formally juxtaposed to Isabeau, leader of the rival armies, and by this means even her excess of purest spirituality is placed fundamentally, if tragically, on a par with the instinctuality of the latter, and equally distinguished from morality in Schiller's meaning of the word. Nothing could be purer and more in accord with the universal law than Johanna's will. Up to the crisis she is, in fact, the Categorical Imperative personified, impervious as she is to the demands of the mood and the moment, to the total living context in which the dictate of the spirit is embedded. Precisely because of that her moral endeavour is a fiasco. In her passionate concern for matters of the spirit she has left the sense side of her being untended. Her sensuality, once roused, turns out to be anarchic, at war with her spirit. The man she loves is the enemy of the universal cause she serves. This moral failure is underscored by her juxtaposition with Sorel. Sorel has no soaring spirituality to compare with Johanna's. But feeling and spirit are *one* and thus her private concern and the general cause coalesce, "Dies Fest des Reichs ist deiner Liebe Fest" (IV.2) and "*Eins* bist du mit der allgemeinen Wonne" (ibid.) as Johanna puts it. Johanna's "Zartgefühl" has here divined a supreme value which has eluded her striving and of which Sorel herself is not conscious: the value of wholeness. Before this value Johanna's ideal of holiness is exposed in its tragic inadequacy. In her identification with the "highest" function and its specific values she has neglected the cultivation of *all* her functions and offended against the only absolute Schiller acknowledges. Johanna's spirituality, like any other constituent function of the psychic organism, taken *per se* is morally neutral. It becomes morally bad when it becomes disengaged from its psychic context; it becomes good, supremely good, when it is organised within that context and reflects and sustains the life quality that belongs to the whole. "Dadurch"—we remember—"dass weniger Kräfte bei ihr thätig waren, wird eine schlimme Handlung schlimm, und so umgekehrt".

Indeed, the tragic inadequacy of moral endeavour is the unchanging theme of the mature dramatist, and every new formulation of it increases the gulf that separates him from Kant. The theme is as it were provisionally formulated in *Maria Stuart* and *Die Braut von Messina*. Elisabeth and Isabella fail, in part at least, because their moral endeavour is vitiated by hypocrisy and presumption. A more rigorous statement of the problem is encountered in *Die Jungfrau von Orleans*, *Demetrius* and *Warbeck*. These three dramas concern themselves with the tragic inadequacy of even the purest endeavour. Johanna and Demetrius fail despite the purity of their moral endeavour, indeed *because* of its very intensity. The tragic irony of such a failure becomes evident from Schiller's note. "Demetrius verschmäht das knechtische Betragen der Russen und spricht davon, dass er es abschaffen werde. *In diesem schönen Zug* liegt der Keim eines unglücklichen Betragens".[1] In *Warbeck*, the problem is taken one step further still. Warbeck is morally vindicated *despite* the lie which flaws his consciousness. Ever more daringly, the ultimate value of

[1] Ibid., xv, p. 558.

the personality is shown to reside in strata which are inaccessible to the moral will, indeed we might say, to consciousness. Ultimate worth lies in an inborn predisposition towards integration, in a felicitous *relation* between the psychic functions rather than in their absolute quality; a natural well-temperedness which no endeavour in the world can create but which moral striving—the activity of the single function—may tragically and incurably disrupt. The outward token of such secret favouredness are beauty, rank and birth—in Schiller's world truer indicators of moral worth than all the purity of will or deed. No striving will make Demetrius what nature did not make him—the born King. No flaw in his striving will take away from Warbeck that innate rightness of nature which is reflected in his regal birth. Only when Johanna returns to the nature she relinquished and from its sources imbibes a new wholesomeness, does she attain the true sublimity that is vouchsafed to her at the end.

Such formulations inevitably recall Schiller's concept of the "Schöne Seele" and indeed the view put forward in *Anmut und Würde* in its entirety. This is as it should be. Yet the conclusions presented here are more than a rephrasing of the familiar notions traditionally associated with this essay. For one thing, I have tried to prove the consistency of Schiller's view of the personality throughout his dramatic poetry as well as his discursive writings—a homogeneity of attitude which has been much disputed. For another—and this is more important—Schiller's argument for totality gains incomparably in cogency and conviction when it is placed in its proper organicistic framework. For it is only when we view the human psyche dynamically as an organism rather than statically as a mere aggregate, and its every constituent as a vital function rather than a mechanical part, that the claim for inclusiveness and totality is seen to be a matter, not of personal inclination, but of strict logical necessity. —And lastly—it is only when we are mindful of the biological slant of Schiller's thinking that we can explain and duly emphasise the curious bias towards the basic physical—even material—endowment of personality which is so marked a feature of the mature thinker's evaluations, both in his poetry and in his theory. In the last resort it is the native endowment that tells—whether we call it beauty, rank, or birth, or grace or genius, or just luck—not what Schiller sums up in the word "Verdienst". And this is not only true for the tragedies. In the *Ästhetische Briefe*, too, there is a slight but unmistakable note of protective partiality in favour of the sense side of our being, our receptivity, as against our intellectual self,[1] a bias that is still perceptible in his assessment of the "Realist" and the "Phantast" at the end of *Über Naive und Sentimentalische Dichtung*. The realist can never become as degraded as the Phantast: for "eben die Natur, der er sich blindlings überliefert, lässt ihn nicht ganz sinken; ihre ewigen Grenzen schützen ihn, ihre unerschöpflichen Hilfsmittel retten ihn, sobald er seine Freiheit nur ohne allen Vorbehalt aufgibt".[2]

These are strange and moving words; the words of a man who has experienced all the ravages of the spirit and who found in nature the uncontaminated source of its renewal. Surely, the ultimate feat of Schiller's idealism lies in the brave recognition that the nature of sublimity is mysteriously and inexorably rooted in the sublimity of nature: a recognition which found eloquent expression in the men and mountains of *Wilhelm Tell*.

[1] Cf. especially the footnotes to letter XIII; *Sämmtliche Schriften*, ed. cit., x. p. 317.

[2] Ibid., x, p. 522.

How far we have moved from the moral cosmos of Kant where reason and consciousness encompass all that is of value in the human existence; and how close to Goethe who believed in "angeborene Verdienste", who confidently asserted that in England he would have been born a lord, and who regarded a ripe old age as a valid form of moral achievement!

I have tried to elucidate the structure of the Schillerian personality and the dramatic world in which it has its being, the conception of the human psyche that underlies this structure, and the criteria of value that are implicit in this conception. But there remains another problem, perhaps the most urgent of all. Granted that Schiller conceives of the human psyche as an organic entity, why should he have rent that total personality, projecting horizontally the hidden strata of the soul and embodying them in a separate being? Why should he have dismembered this personality as he saw it and distributed its several functions over a number of individuals, each a fragment and only together forming a person?

The answer to this question is the key to Schiller's peculiar genius. His technique of externalisation enabled him to attain two ends by one and the same operation: the maximal amount of reality and the maximal amount of poetic truth. For what is the empirical reality which is the material of his poetry?

The poet himself answers this question in the 6th *Ästhetische Brief*. Comparing Greek humanity with modernity he says "Wie ganz anders bei uns Neuern! Auch bei uns ist das Bild der Gattung in den Individuen vergrössert auseinandergewofen—aber in Bruchstücken, nicht in veränderten Mischungen, dass man von Individuum zu Individuum herumfragen muss, um die Totalität der Gattung zusammenzulesen. Bei uns, möchte man fast versucht werden zu behaupten, äussern sich die Gemütskräfte auch in der Erfahrung so getrennt, wie der

Psychologe sie in der Vorstellung scheidet, und wir sehen nicht bloss einzelne Subjekte, sondern ganze Klassen von Menschen nur einen Teil ihrer Anlagen entfalten, während dass die übrigen, wie bei verkrüppelten Gewächsen, kaum mit matter Spur angedeutet sind".[1]

The psychological justification for the technique of externalisation, Schiller tells us, lies in the predicament of his age, which is now commonly recognised as the predicament of our era, of western civilisation. It lies in the fragmentation of the human psyche through the twin forces of mechanisation and specialisation which in time have brought about the disintegration of its close-knit structure into a haphazard assembly of isolated functions, some highly prized and differentiated, others neglected or even repressed.[2] All the characteristic features we noted in the tragedies are reflected in this passage. Here, as there, we have the telling metaphor of a maimed organism, of one luxuriating function usurping the life of the whole and doomed, in the last resort, to die: For unless it be regenerated the "verkrüppelte Gewächs" must perish as inevitably as the partial personality.

The technique of externalisation then is Schiller's way of articulating in inherently dramatic terms and with great immediacy reality as he experienced it: the reality of a specialist civilisation. But it needs to achieve more than that, and it does achieve more. For this reality as he felt it, as we feel it, is not tractable to art. Art, Schiller tells us in his profound essay on Matthisson's poems, must be concerned with the pure object, that is, with the

1 ed. cit., x. p. 289.

2 For an excellent discussion of this development in modern psychological terms cf. C. G. Jung, *Psychologische Typen* (Ibid. II. pp. 97-189). Zürich, Leipzig and Stuttgart, 1925.

object apprehended in its typical generic form. And this pure object must in turn be apprehended through the medium of a pure subjectivity. In this interpenetration of a pure objectivity and a pure subjectivity in the artistic act lies the secret of the communicability of art. But the fragmented modern individual is as far from being the typical human personality as the "verkrüppelte Gewächs" is from being a typical representative of its species. In the essay "*Über das Pathetische*" Schiller has elucidated the artistic processes by which these given human materials can be made aesthetically tractable. Here, as always, the task is to strip the "wirkliche Fall' of its particular determinations and accidental trappings, of those "Zufälligkeiten und Nebendinge" that cluster around it, and to reveal the pure generic object within. Now, the generic character of man, Schiller argues, is the possession of a will. "Der Mensch ist das Wesen, welches will". In empirical reality—the reality with which Schiller deals in the *Ästhetische Briefe*—this will is always determined one way or another. Men are in fact placed into a living context which is as limiting as it is concrete. The dramatist's job, in line with that of any artist, is to recover this quintessential man, "das Wesen welches will", from the welter of his actual determinations. This he does, not so much by denying that his hero is in fact a fully determinate character—to do so would be to evade reality rather than to transmute it—but by concentrating our attention on the capacity to will as such, rather than on any specific determination of his volition, and by extenuating and enhancing this aspect of indeterminacy by any means in his power.[1] By this shift of focus, what is generic in the human character is sorted out from what is particular and empirically limited, and

1 This artistic operation had already been fully described in *Über den Grund des Vergnügens an tragischen Gegenständen*. Cf. *Sämmtliche Schriften*, ed. cit., x. p. 15, 11, 5ff.

the aesthetic propensities of the dramatist's material—man—are brought into play. Thus *Über das Pathetische*.

What better means of performing this crucial switch of attention could Schiller have devised than the prismatic refracting of the human psyche into its elements through the device of externalisation? The tragic hero, embodiment of the rational functions, is all but unaware of the elemental drives which, although suppressed, do in fact coerce him. This dynamic side of his being is embodied and articulated in the separate being of the antagonist, a figure that is as fully determinate and deeply enmeshed in necessity as the protagonist deems himself to be indeterminate and free. We might say that he lives out the compulsion which the tragic hero denies. Maria Stuart's rival is in fact determined by deeply buried elemental impulses. It is "Die wilde Glut verstohlner Lüste" in her which draws her into the fatal encounter with the younger Queen. But it is in the figure of Maria, throughout the play associated with the imagery of fire, that these determining motives are embodied and revealed in their full coercive force. The tragic protagonists themselves—Elisabeth, Wallenstein, Fiesco, Posa, Isabella, cut off as they are from their deeper drives, deem themselves completely free from the contingencies of their concrete situation. To this presumed freedom of will they cling, delighting in the contemplation of the full range of their powers rather than in the exercise of any one of them.

Psychologically speaking, this image of himself as an indeterminate being which the tragic hero communicates, is a delusion. Judging from an over-all point of view of the work of art, however, it is an indispensable illusion which engenders his aesthetic potency and the potency of the composition of which he is the centre. For he presents himself as "das Wesen welches will", as man in his generic aspect. Through this faulty apprehension of himself he becomes—an aesthetic object.[1]

Thus the technique of externalisation accomplishes in one operation the two fundamental, and—it would seem—contrary artistic processes. On the one hand, it enables the poet to articulate a deeply personal and deeply felt experience: the experience of modern man as a tragically one-sided being. On the other hand, it enables him to transmute these raw materials of experience into art. For by externalising the real determinate character of his hero in the separate character of the antagonist, he does justice to the full force of reality. At the same time he is left free to develop his central figure in its pure aesthetic semblance, and to create a symbolic being which exfoliates in sovereign disregard of all but its own poetic laws.

Undoubtedly Schiller knew what he was doing. In a letter to Goethe he stresses the fact "Dass alle poetischen Personen symbolische Wesen sind, dass sie, als poetische Gestalten immer das Allgemeine der Menschheit darzustellen und auszusprechen haben" and he only urges "dass der Dichter sowie der Künstler überhaupt auf eine öffentliche und ehrliche Art von der Wirklichkeit sich entfernen und daran erinnern soll, dass er es thut" . . .[1] And in the 16th aesthetic letter we find a passage which it is difficult not to read as an exact description and assessment of the crucial technique he has employed in his drama from the first and will use to the last. The artist makes use of his supreme right—Schiller writes—"wenn er den Schein von dem Wesen zurücknimmt und mit demselben nach eignen Gesetzen schaltet . . . je sorgfältiger er die Gestalt von dem Wesen trennt, und je

1 For a discussion of the precise aesthetic function of the contemplativeness of Schiller's protagonists, cf. my article Reflection as a Function of Form, *Publications of the English Goethe Society*, Vol. XXIV, 1955, p. 1-32.

2 *Sämmtliche Schriften*, ed. cit., X. p. 372.

mehr Selbstständigkeit er derselben zu geben weiss, desto mehr wird er nicht bloss das Reich der Schönheit erweitern, sondern selbst die Grenzen der Wahrheit bewahren; denn er kann den Schein nicht von der Wirklichkeit reinigen, ohne zugleich die Wirklichkeit von dem Schein frey zu machen".[1]

You will see that the technique of Externalisation—the refraction of the human psyche into its basic elements and the independent poetic exploration of the aesthetically more fruitful constituent—led the poet into uncharted artistic regions far beyond the familiar bounds of representational dramatic portraiture, and afforded him deep insights into the nature and possibilities of his medium. How bold and exploratory Schiller's dramatic art is has not, I think, been fully appreciated; nor are we sufficiently alive to the formidable realism of his thinking on matters moral and spiritual, on the human condition and its cure. This quality derives from the unswerving organicistic slant of his mind, and it is this which constitutes his deepest affinity with Goethe and with the thought of our day. For Schiller and Goethe were united in a quest which concerns us still: the quest for an organic structure of the personality, so that, far from falling behind nature in her physical creations and reverting to a state of inner anarchy, we attain to a higher, a conscious mode of integration and, in so doing, free the deepest springs of our creativeness.

It is indeed my hope that these reflections may have done something to bring Schiller closer to us; to remind us that he formulates a basic contemporary predicament and contemporary aspirations in a contemporary artistic idiom; that, born 200 years ago, he is a very great child of our time.

[1] *Schillers Briefe*, ed. Jonas. Stuttgart, Leipzig, Berlin, Wien, 1892-96, vol. v, p. 418.

SCHILLER: REFLECTIONS ON A BICENTENARY

By W. Witte

AMONG the books which accompanied Carlyle's first letters to Goethe was his *Life of Schiller*. This work, first published serially in the *London Magazine*, had appeared in book form in 1825, twenty years after Schiller's death; it had been Carlyle's first original publication, and it is the earliest monograph on Schiller of any lasting value. Carlyle sent it to Goethe, along with some of his translations from the German, by way of introducing himself to one—to quote his own words—"whom I never saw, yet whose voice came to me from afar, with counsel and help, in my utmost need".[1] The gift was well received, and a few years later Goethe wrote a brief but weighty introduction to a German version of Carlyle's book. He also sent Carlyle a complete set of his Correspondence with Schiller, the concluding volumes of which had just appeared in print. Schiller thus figures from the start in the Goethe-Carlyle correspondence, an exchange of views which gave Goethe an opportunity of elaborating one of his favourite ideas, the idea of world literature—much to Carlyle's delight, who felt fortified in his own convictions by what Goethe had to say on the subject. "National literature", Goethe remarked in conversation with Eckermann,[2] "does not mean much nowadays; the epoch of world literature is due, and everyone must now endeavour to hasten its coming". People from different countries, Goethe felt, could be led to a better understanding of each other by familiarizing themselves with what is best in

1 15 April, 1827.

2 31 January, 1827.

the poets and writers of all nations. This does not mean that Goethe was advocating a colourless cosmopolitanism: far from it. He insists, on the contrary, that national peculiarities must be respected and studied. At the same time he maintains that such study will reveal significant affinities. "It is clear", he writes to Carlyle,[1] "that the efforts of the best poets and creative writers everywhere have for some considerable time been directed towards what is common to all mankind. In each individual work . . . that universal element may be seen shining ever more clearly through what is national and personal . . . It is the hallmark of true merit that it belongs to humanity as a whole". By taking their stand upon this common ground, people of different race and language can learn from each other and can learn to tolerate, perhaps even to like, each other. When Goethe consented to launch the German version of Carlyle's *Life of Schiller* with an introduction from his own pen, his purpose was to lend the prestige of his name to a book which provided welcome confirmation of his own views.

One is reminded of Goethe's idea of world literature whenever some special occasion, such as an anniversary, calls for commemoration and reappraisal of an author's achievement, not only among his fellow-countrymen but in other countries as well. The bicentenary of Schiller's birth is such an occasion; and one feels prompted to ask, with Schiller in mind: have we advanced towards the goal which Goethe envisaged?—In one sense, a great deal of progress has undoubtedly been made. One can point to the spread of German studies in Britain, paralleled by an even more spectacular growth of English studies in Germany since Goethe's day: a process which has gone on, virtually unchecked, in spite of two major wars between the two countries. Nowadays Schiller's

[1] 20 July, 1827.

works occupy a safe and prominent place in the German curricula of British schools and universities. There is, moreover, the growing volume of publications in English on various aspects of Schiller, including new editions and translations. The Institute of Germanic Languages and Literatures, which arranged a Schiller exhibition to mark the bicentenary, and the English Goethe Society, which has always paid due attention to Goethe's friend and partner, are further vindications of Goethe's prophecy. All this must be entered on the credit side of the account. But it may be argued that these things, important and heartening though they are, represent the efforts of specialists who take a professional interest in German literature in general and in Schiller in particular, and that they do not noticeably affect the bulk of the educated reading public, let alone that elusive character, the man in the street. The general reader's attitude to Schiller was recently summed up—not unfairly—by Philip Toynbee, in a review of Thomas Mann's *Last Essays* (which include his Schiller essay of 1955). "The English", Toynbee writes, "have never, I think, been very much interested in Schiller, and it is not very likely that Mann's dutiful and affectionate essay will induce them to pay him more attention. We know that he *must* be a great writer, but we find it hard to respond to his fervent sublimities".[1] In this attitude of indifference tinged with mockery, the average British reader has been to some extent encouraged by critics and literary historians, some of whom have been a little hasty in writing Schiller off as a wasting asset in the balance-sheet of German literature. If, for instance, a reader turns for information on Schiller to the major work of general reference in the English language, the *Encyclopædia Britannica*, he finds, even in the current issue, an article, written some considerable time ago by the late J. G. Robertson, which ends as

1 *The Observer*, 26 April, 1959.

follows: "In point of fact, Schiller's genius lacks that universality which characterizes Goethe's; as a dramatist, a philosopher, an historian, and a lyric poet, he was the exponent of ideas which belong essentially to the Europe of the period before the French revolution". Having taken this judgment on trust (and what else can he do?), the reader may be forgiven if he does not choose to put Schiller very high on his list of priorities and if he refuses to take any particular interest in the Schiller bicentenary. If challenged, he would probably say, with a shrug, "Why should I? If the Germans want to commemorate this bicentenary, that is their affair. They are in any case much more anniversary-conscious: by all means let them enjoy themselves in their own way. But why should *we* bother with Schiller?"

Put like that, the question may sound a little crude. Nevertheless it is a fair question and deserves to be taken seriously. The reader of to-day is faced with many claims on his time, and he is entitled to ask why it would be worth his while to acquaint himself with a foreign author who was born two hundred years ago. It may not be possible to give a brief answer; but assuming that the questioner is prepared to listen, it ought to be possible to give a reasonably plain one.

J. G. Robertson's view will serve as a starting-point. "As a dramatist", Robertson asserts, "as a philosopher, an historian, and a lyric poet, Schiller was the exponent of ideas which belong essentially to the Europe of the period before the French revolution". This is a view which was fairly widely held some fifty years ago; but one may say, without disrespect to those who held it then, that it has been proved wrong by the passage of time. It has been said that Schiller is outmoded, a period piece, an eighteenth century worthy, left high and dry by the tide of events: but all that does not square with the impression one gets when one reads Schiller to-day. What strikes one again and again in Schiller's writings—in his plays, his poems, his historical and philosophical prose—is their relevance to the events and problems, political, social, and spiritual, of our own age. It is true that this modernity is sometimes veiled, in his prose and in his verse, by a manner which differs from the current idiom of to-day and which some people find over-emphatic, too rhetorical, too explicit, and generally uncongenial. But as soon as one becomes attuned to Schiller's style (which, as style, is by no means without its merits!), one discovers that the things he writes about are precisely the things that concern us most at the present time.

(It is not being suggested, of course, that this modernity in itself makes Schiller a great poet or a great dramatist. One may dispute the allegation that a poet's ideas are out of date while admitting, at the same time, that those ideas as such have no poetic worth; "they have that worth"—to quote A. C. Bradley[1]—"only when, passing through the unity of the poet's being, they reappear as qualities of imagination, and then are indeed mighty powers in the world of poetry".)

The modernity of Schiller's ideas may be illustrated—to take a concrete example—by reference to the social revolution of our era. In this country that revolution has mercifully been a peaceful and bloodless one, but it has wrought great changes, all the same. It has brought us the welfare state, which undertakes to shield its citizens from want and provides them, as of right, with a wide range of social services. Schiller, who had known hard times himself, was well aware of the needs of the underprivileged; in the distich *Würde des Menschen* he

[1] A. C. Bradley, *Oxford Lectures on Poetry*, London, 1909, p. 7.

insists that those needs have first priority:

> Nichts mehr davon, ich bitt euch. Zu essen gebt ihm, zu wohnen;
> Habt ihr die Blösse bedeckt, gibt sich die Würde von selbst.

Thomas Mann comments on these lines in his Schiller essay, and pretends to be horrified: "But that's socialist materialism, Heaven help us!" Is it not remarkable that an aphorism of Schiller's—whose ideas are alleged to be all pre-French-Revolution—should prompt such a comment? Socialist materialism: with that phrase Thomas Mann projects Schiller into the great political debate of our own century. Would Schiller have opted for the eastern side of the Iron Curtain in the Germany of to-day? If the opinion of the most accomplished literary critic of the Marxist school is anything to go by, he would not have been very acceptable there. Georg Lukács sees Schiller as a writer who failed, rather disappointingly, to live up to the revolutionary promise of his early works; as a potential revolutionary force, Lukács maintains, Schiller was spent even before the outbreak of the French Revolution, and when that great challenge came, he was therefore incapable of taking the correct party line.[1] It is entertaining to observe that Lukács, like J. G. Robertson, seeks to relegate Schiller to the period before the French Revolution: J. G. Robertson would surely have found Lukács a disturbing bedfellow. No less diverting is the intellectual tightrope act performed by the literary experts of East Germany, who censure Schiller for his shortcomings as a revolutionary, for his regrettable failure to anticipate the Marxian dialectic, and in the same breath claim him as their own, a prophet of world socialism. In a manifesto published by the official "Schiller Committee" of the East German Republic, the authors deplore Schiller's idealist philosophy,

[1] Georg Lukács, *Goethe und seine Zeit*, Berne, 1947, pp. 54, 87 f., 109. Cf. W. Witte, "Law and the Social Order in Schiller's Thought", in *Schiller and Burns and Other Essays*, Oxford, 1959, pp. 67 ff.

which they stigmatize as mere escapism; at the same time they declare that Schiller's works are the rightful property of the German working class, who receive authoritative guidance in matters of interpretation from the Central Committee of their party.[1] Those who do not subscribe to the Marxist orthodoxy will feel sceptical about such *ex cathedra* pronouncements. One thing is certain: Schiller could never have accepted a political doctrine and a theory of social evolution which are based on a strictly materialist philosophy, for this would have run counter to his deepest convictions. The economic structure of society, the distribution of wealth, the relief of poverty, measures designed to prevent exploitation of one section of the community by another—all these things are important, as Schiller knew very well; so important, in fact, that they must take pride of place in any scheme of social reform. If a man is hungry, homeless, in rags, if his family are in want, it is no use talking to him about the things of the spirit: any missionary knows that. The first thing to do is to relieve his pressing needs. But priority in time does not necessarily imply precedence in a scale of values. The only ultimate guarantee of social progress, Schiller holds,[2] lies in the hearts and minds of the individual men and women who make up the community. The essential task, therefore, is the education of the individual citizen. At a critical moment in *Wallenstein*,[3] the hero says "Es ist der Geist, der sich den Körper baut". It was an article of faith with Schiller that the spirit of man can triumph over the material conditions of his existence.[4] One can see that faith at work in Schiller's own life, in his deter-

1 "Erklärung des Schiller-Komitees der Deutschen Demokratischen Republik", 1959.

2 Letter to Prince Friedrich Christian of Holstein-Augustenburg, 13 July, 1793.

3 *Wallensteins Tod*, III, 13, l. 1813.

4 Five weeks before his death he reaffirmed this conviction in his last letter to Wilhelm von Humboldt, 2 April, 1805.

mined struggle against ill-health and other discouragements; and what he had put to the test of personal experience he applied, all the more confidently, in his political thinking.

Schiller insists uncompromisingly on the importance and the rights of the individual. The state, he holds, is a means to an end; it exists to create conditions which will enable its individual citizens to lead full and satisfying lives. In order to achieve that purpose, political authority is necessary; and at once the question arises—how is the individual to be safeguarded against possible encroachments of authority? Having delegated power, how can he be sure that this power will not be abused? Although this is one of the perennial problems of political theory and practice, it is of special importance at the present time, when totalitarian conceptions of society are challenging the parliamentary democracies on all hands, and when even in those liberal democracies individual freedom is curbed by the kind of benevolent regimentation which is the price we have to pay for the benefits of the welfare state. Schiller would have been quite at home in the politics of our time. He had come up against the arbitrary use of power early in life, in his conflict with his sovereign, Duke Karl Eugen of Württemberg. Painful though that experience had been at the time, it proved an immensely formative one; it was one of those decisive experiences in a man's life which determine the direction of his interests and the way his mind works. Throughout his life Schiller was fascinated by the problem of power; the majority of his plays deal with it in one way or another. In his first tragedy, the young hero with his band of outlaws rebels against all established authority, only to discover, in the end, that however corrupt the existing order may be, mere anarchy does not offer a workable alternative. Karl Moor's rebellion in *Die Räuber* is only a very minor one; he gives the authorities a great deal of trouble, but he never has any real chance of seizing the reins of government, nor has he any desire to do so. However, the figure of the fully fledged dictator is not long in coming. In Schiller's second drama, the subtitle of which proclaims it a political play—"A Republican Tragedy"—we have a real *coup d'état;* the hero, Fiesco, contrives to overthrow the government of the city state of Genoa, though he does not live to enjoy his success. (That, at any rate, is what happens in the more convincing version of the play). Fiesco is killed in the very hour of his triumph because the chief spokesman of republican sentiment will not tolerate a usurper who is guided by selfish ambition: compelled to choose between two evils—viz., two autocrats—he decides that if he cannot have government by the people, he would rather reinstate the old ruler, who is at least a man of proved integrity. Though Fiesco is richly endowed with gifts of leadership, his motives are suspect, and his bid for power therefore deserves to fail. This theme of "ambition in action, and ultimately defeated"[1] is taken up again in *Wallenstein*, a profound and penetrating study of a would-be dictator in which the playwright explores the lure and the perils of power. Here is political adventure on the grand scale, undertaken by a man of truly commanding stature who has some cause to think of himself as the Man of Destiny. What he is plotting is nothing less than high treason; by joining forces with the enemy he hopes to make himself the arbiter of the Empire. But, Wallenstein reflects (as others have reflected since), are there not cases in political life where success is its own justification, both in the eyes of contemporaries and in the judgment of posterity; when a crime against the state, having succeeded, is seen in a new perspective in which it no longer appears as a crime but as a creative act of political renewal? Was Caesar not flouting the law when he crossed

1 Cf. Schiller's letter to W. H. von Dalberg, 16 November, 1782.

the Rubicon? "Gib mir sein Glück", Wallenstein says, "das andre will ich tragen": "that other thing" being the censure of men and the judgment of God. Wallenstein is so completely mesmerized by the thought of his own greatness that he loses touch with his fellow-men, whom he sees merely as pawns in his own game, forgetting that they have minds and principles of their own. Nor does he acknowledge any moral law that transcends mere human conventions. Although he has a strong sense of the supernatural, of fate—he keeps an astrologer in his entourage, he casts horoscopes, he scans the heavens for a propitious conjunction of the planets—Wallenstein has no sense of the divine: he is not conscious of any need of grace or any fear of damnation. In this respect he differs radically from Macbeth, with whom he has often been compared and with whom he has otherwise much in common. Two quotations may serve to point the contrast. Both are expressions of defiance, the words of men who pit themselves against the world, and they are thus superficially similar; but this resemblance only serves to emphasize the profound difference in outlook which they reveal. Macbeth is constantly aware of another world beyond the temporal one, a world with which he knows he must come to terms, however determined he may be that for his own good here and now all causes shall give way.

> If 't be so,
> For Banquo's issue have I fil'd my mind;
> For them the gracious Duncan have I murther'd;
> Put rancours in the vessel of my peace,
> Only for them; and mine eternal jewel
> Given to the common Enemy of man,
> To make them kings, the seed of Banquo kings!
> Rather than so, come, fate, into the list,
> And champion me to th' utterance!

Macbeth is thinking of his immortal soul—"mine eternal jewel"—and of its fate in the world to come. And

Wallenstein? At the moment of decision he exclaims:

> Doch eh ich sinke in die Nichtigkeit,
> So klein aufhöre, der so gross begonnen,
> Eh mich die Welt mit jenen Elenden
> Verwechselt, die der Tag erschafft und stürzt,
> Eh spreche Welt und Nachwelt meinen Namen
> Mit Abscheu aus, und Friedland sei die Losung
> Für jede fluchenswerte Tat.

Although Wallenstein uses the language of eschatology—"each accursed deed"—he uses it in a purely conventional way. He is thinking, not of the last things, but of the position which he believes to be his due, and of his fame: he would rather be remembered with hate and dread than not be remembered at all. His thoughts are bounded by the temporal world, its prizes and its valuations.

The problem of protecting the liberty of the subject against the arbitrary use of power arises in its most acute form under a dictatorship, but it may arise in different circumstances too. An established hereditary monarchy may harden into despotism. That is what happens in Schiller's *Don Carlos*. In the Spain of the Counter-Reformation, two young idealists "form the project of realizing the happiest conditions attainable to human society",[1] but they perish in their attempt to subvert the despotic powers of Church and State: the liberation of the Netherlands which they had been planning will have to be achieved by other means. A happier ending awaits the reader of *Wilhelm Tell:* a small nation which is being drawn into the orbit of a larger power until it is in danger of becoming a satellite state resists political intimidation and asserts its independence.

The Swiss in *Wilhelm Tell* rise in defence of their chartered rights which have been set aside. They are not lawless people; they know that only the rule of law makes it possible for men to avoid the extremes of anarchy

1 *Briefe über Don Carlos*, 8th Letter.

on the one hand and tyranny on the other. But how can the rule of law be enforced in international affairs? What happens when considerations of right and wrong are bedevilled—as they usually are in international disputes—by power politics, national sentiment and rival ideologies, when there is no supreme court of arbitration, when the parties insist on being judges in their own cause, and when the law thus becomes an instrument of policy? The search for a solution of this problem is the major theme of world politics to-day. Schiller has no solution to offer; what he does give us, in *Maria Stuart*, is an acute and most exciting analysis. When the play opens, the law has spoken: Mary Queen of Scots is under sentence of death, having been tried and found guilty by a special tribunal composed of the first peers of the realm, and Lord Burleigh arrives at Fotheringhay to apprize her of the verdict. Mary, however, immediately denies the competence of the court. She came to England seeking sanctuary, and her royal birth and status, she claims, confer upon her the privilege of exterritoriality: she is not subject to the jurisdiction of any English court, however constituted. Burleigh rejoins that neither the right of asylum nor the status of the refugee can ever sanction subversive political agitation or attempts on the life of the sovereign, and that such crimes against the state must obviously be dealt with according to the law of the country in which they were committed. Mary counters these arguments by pointing out that her complicity in Babington's plot against the life of Elizabeth has not been conclusively proved according to the rules of English legal procedure because she has never been confronted with the principal witnesses for the prosecution. As for her subversive activities—what her antagonists would have called the interference of her foreign sympathizers in the internal affairs of England—she argues that she has been unlawfully restrained and that she was entitled to seek redress by rallying her friends abroad to her support. Here she invokes one of the basic principles of natural law, the right of legitimate self-defence, of meeting unlawful force by force. And when Burleigh gravely reminds her that an appeal to force is not likely to benefit a prisoner, he gives her the opening she needs to wind up her case. She is only too well aware that Elizabeth has her in her power and can have her executed: all she has to do is to confirm the sentence of the tribunal by adding her signature. But if she does so, Mary declares, it will be an act of naked force which no specious show of legality can mask. With admirable skill Schiller reveals the ambiguities inherent in a dispute of this kind, when statesmen talk in terms of justice but think in terms of expediency and when the distinction between the administration of the law and the exercise of power becomes blurred. Goethe once remarked that Schiller had the makings of a great statesman; one may add that although as a youngster he was not attracted to the study of law (for which he had originally been destined), he had the makings of a brilliant lawyer too.

English and Scottish theatre-goers had an opportunity of seeing *Maria Stuart* in the autumn of 1958, when, as a kind of prelude to the bicentenary, two different productions of the play ran in London and in Edinburgh. At the Edinburgh Festival, a company of actors from the Old Vic staged a new abridged English version by Stephen Spender, which they subsequently presented to London audiences at their own theatre in the Waterloo Road. About the same time a German company—the Düsseldorfer Schauspielhaus—performed the play in the original at Sadler's Wells. Performances of Schiller's plays are rare in this country; two productions of the same play, put on in quick succession by two leading professional companies, must be a unique event in the annals of the British stage. What did critics and audiences make of this unfamiliar experience? The critical reception was mixed—genuinely enthusiastic in one or two cases, merely polite in others, and now and then somewhat patronizing. The play being a historical one, English critics could not help comparing it with Shakespeare's histories. Kenneth Tynan, writing in the *Observer*,[1] remarks that "Schiller's play, the Vic's first non-Shakespearean excursion for half a decade, illustrates only too aptly the extent to which Shakespeare's histories defy emulation and dwarf competition"; and Alan Brien, of the *Spectator*, calls *Mary Stuart* "a soupy Shakespeare-and-soda decanted from Schiller by Stephen Spender",[2] though he goes on to say, in the same notice, that the play "should not be condemned as second-hand Shakespeare".[3] The same critic's strictures on the Düsseldorf company's performance are tempered by his admission that "for the non-German-speaking audience, the music of the language is lost".[4] The Edinburgh performance provoked a lively controversy in the correspondence columns of the *Scotsman*. Some members of the public took the playwright to task for having departed from the recorded facts of Scottish history; others rallied to his defence, and got the better of the argument. All this is worth recording because it testifies to the enduring vitality of the work. Here is a play which deals with live issues and which, after a century and a half, can still spark off controversy. No doubt this is what attracted Mr. Spender to the task of producing a

1 7 September, 1958.

2 *The Spectator*, 19 September, 1958.

3 While agreeing whole-heartedly with this conclusion, one may have certain reservations about the arguments which are adduced in support of it. In the Shakespearian history plays, Alan Brien writes, "there is too often a depressing shortage of sex among the court cards. But *Mary Stuart* revolves around sex—it is almost a study in two types of nymphomania".

4 *The Spectator*, 3 October, 1958.

new English version. In an article on the two performances—the Old Vic one and the German one—he writes:[1] "There is a vision of the rôle of necessity in history, and a horror of the corruption of power, and these are relevant to a contemporary audience".

In the same article, Mr. Spender draws attention to another quality that appealed to him. "In spite of the cry 'this is not poetry'—has not totally unambiguous, intellectual yet unobscure, rhythmic language, a lesson which poets to-day might pay heed to?" "In spite of the cry 'this is not poetry' ": it seems a strange thing to say about a National Bard. Yet the cry has been raised, and is apt to be raised more insistently in an age when sense in poetry is at a discount. Just as in sculpture and painting many artists of our time have decided to dispense with any representation of recognisable objects, so in much present-day poetry the propositional element of speech, the statement and development of ideas, has been eliminated or much reduced. Such poetry does not seek to convey a definable meaning but rather to cast a spell; it relies for its effect on symbolism, on echoes and contrasts in sound, on ambiguities, on the incantation of rhythm, on the emotive overtones of words and phrases, and on an elaborate network of sub-conscious association. It does not set out to imitate anything, to re-create and deepen experiences with which we are familiar in our everyday world; on the contrary, it endeavours to alienate us from that world and to create a world of its own. It asks, not to be "understood" in the usual sense of that word, but to be responded to. Work of this kind is often baffling, and may even appear absurd, because it does not lend itself to rational analysis. Some people are inclined to lament this trend in contemporary art because, they argue, it makes art freakish, esoteric, and irresponsible, and thus cuts it off from the life of the

1 *The New Statesman*, 4 October, 1958.

community. Such complaints, however, are useless. Artists and poets must have a free hand, and it is futile to blame them for doing what they feel impelled to do: to criticize Dylan Thomas, for instance, or indeed T. S. Eliot, because they do not write with the elegant lucidity of Pope or the smooth flow of Tennyson; or, to take German examples, to condemn Karl Krolow or Ingeborg Bachmann because they do not write in the manner of Heine or Eichendorff. At the same time, it should be borne in mind that the present vogue of irrationality does not invalidate poetry written in a more rational manner. Such poetry may not be in the current fashion; but if it is wrong to reject the new merely because it appears cryptic and bizarre, it is equally wrong to disparage the old merely because it is unfashionable. Schiller is a case in point. He is a reflective, highly self-conscious poet; the impulse behind his best poetry is predominantly intellectual, and he has the gift of expressing his ideas in verse of remarkable lucidity and force which, at its best, achieves what Thomas Mann has called "classical popularity". Schiller himself defined this kind of popularity—the only kind worth striving for—in his review of Bürger's poems. "If a poem can stand the scrutiny of true taste, and if it combines with this advantage the kind of clarity and intelligibility which enable it to live on the lips of the people, then it bears upon it the seal of perfection". This quality, it may be observed in passing, Schiller shared with his coeval Robert Burns. However far-fetched a comparison of the two poets may appear at first sight, they both possess the rare and precious gift of bringing poetry within the range of the common man without debasing it. And this is to our present purpose; for what makes Schiller accessible, as a poet, to a wide and mixed public among his compatriots also makes him accessible to the non-German reader. In German literature, as in other literatures, there are poets whose work is virtually inaccessible to all but a very few foreign readers: those few, that is, who have not merely a competent scholarly command of the poet's language (that in itself is not enough) but who have lived in it, who have made it part of themselves, so that its words and sounds and forms have come to evoke in them the same range of associations as are evoked in the native speaker. The majority, finding themselves nonplussed, might appropriately quote St. Paul: "except ye utter by the tongue words easy to be understood, how shall it be known what is spoken?" To such readers Schiller offers a foothold, at least, in the domain of German poetry; a limited foothold, it is true, but a secure one.

A poet of genius, Schiller declares,[1] should resolve the most sublime philosophy of life into simple natural sentiments, make the results of laborious research available to the imagination and, with the aid of imagery that is readily grasped, enable simple minds to divine the secrets of the thinker. In his own poems he put these precepts into practice; some of them contain the quintessence of his philosophical and critical thinking, transmuted into poetic utterance. These poems thus provide a key to that part of Schiller's *œuvre* which probably appeals least to the non-specialist: his writings on aesthetics. The English-speaking reader in particular is not likely to be spontaneously attracted to these writings, for he does not like his aesthetics neat. He prefers practical, applied criticism to what Saintsbury calls "metacriticism", i.e., general theoretical reflections on questions of art. Nor is he to be blamed for his preference. Some of Schiller's essays, one must admit, look a little forbidding. And yet their message is fundamentally simple. They affirm the importance of art—taking the word in its widest sense—in the life of modern man. Schiller holds that aesthetic

1 *Über Bürgers Gedichte.*

experience can save us from the besetting danger of modern life, the disintegration of the human personality. If that danger was felt to be formidable in Schiller's time, it certainly cannot be said to have receded since; and there are passages in the sixth of his *Letters on the Aesthetic Education of Man* which show that he foresaw what lay ahead. In bygone ages of faith, men's lives were securely centred in their religion. In an increasingly secular society that sheet-anchor is gone; and what is there to take its place? Science, the great idol of our technological era, is a silent goddess, beyond good and evil, who will not or cannot tell us how to ensure the one and avoid the other. Thrown back upon themselves, men find that their inward resources are threatened by an insidious process of erosion. In any highly mechanized civilisation, it becomes more and more difficult for a man to be himself, to preserve his individuality intact; where the pattern of government puts a premium on conformity, the difficulty is greater still. Men are thought of, and tend to think of themselves, in terms of statistics, as units in some sort of classifiable group: as producers or consumers, for instance, or as employees, as voters, as members of a trade union, as insurance risks, as rate-payers, as motorists or pedestrians—in short, as entries on a variety of index files, material for electronic computers. This depersonalized character of modern society means a fragmentation of human existence; more particularly, Schiller argues, it tends to dissociate man's reasoning faculty from his moral and emotional life. By reducing him to a function of a complicated social equation it deprives him of his freedom, and with his freedom he loses something of his human stature and his human dignity. Men thus partly dehumanized cannot in the long run maintain the society which has brought them to this pass. In his poem *Der Spaziergang*, Schiller describes in some memorable lines the collapse of an advanced, complex, highly sophisticated civilisation which, for all the glamour of its outward appearance, is rotten at the heart. Schiller likens it to a building hollowed out by decay; though it still presents an imposing façade, it crumbles under the relentless touch of time. One is reminded of a scriptural parallel—the story of the foolish man who built his house on sand, "and the rains descended, and the floods came, and the winds blew, and beat upon that house; and it fell: and great was the fall of it". Such parallels (which often suggest themselves as one reads Schiller) show that his concern for the quality of the individual human life is also the concern of the Christian moralist. More they do not prove. To suggest, as some have done, that Schiller is an evangelist *manqué*, a sort of unlicensed preacher of the gospel, is to misrepresent a thinker who deserves to be met on his own ground and to turn a blind eye to the fundamentals of Christian doctrine.

One may agree that there is not much wrong with Schiller's diagnosis of our modern malaise: but what of the cure? As a young medical practitioner Schiller is said to have favoured very drastic prescriptions, and he certainly acted on the same principle of "kill or cure" when he was treating himself during his first serious illness in 1783. But when it is a question of prescribing for the body politic, his method is quite different. What he recommends in this case is no shock therapy, no shot in the arm, but a protracted and exacting course of treatment which aims at nothing less than a complete regeneration of the patient. The interaction between man's physical nature and his spiritual self preoccupied Schiller even in his student days (it was the subject of his thesis of 1780); he was well aware that mental and emotional disturbances may produce physical symptoms, which can be removed by restoring the patient's psychic balance. The malady of modern man is of this psychosomatic kind, and Schiller accordingly advocates psychotherapy. In aesthetic experience, he argues, man's split personality once more coheres; our emotions, our senses, and our intellect all come into play, but they no longer conflict. In responding to a work of art, we respond with the whole of our undivided nature. This total response is wholly self-sufficient, and its own justification; in making it, we are not trying to achieve anything, we are not prompted by any ulterior motives but engaging in a disinterested activity, and while it lasts we are released from the bondage of our passions and desires and from the goad of our aggressive or acquisitive instincts: we are made whole, and we are set free.

If one is prepared to take this theory of Schiller's seriously, then it may be argued that now is the time when it should be possible to test it empirically. Schiller's idea of making the enjoyment of art in all its forms an integral part of people's daily lives is much more of a practical proposition now than it was in Schiller's lifetime. If technical progress has left us diseased, it has on the other hand produced some novel means of applying the antidote which Schiller recommends. Sound broadcasting and gramophone records have made music and poetry readily accessible to millions of listeners; television and the cinema are bringing their own form of drama or narrative to similarly vast audiences. Modern travel facilities enable people to see masterpieces of art and architecture at home and abroad. Improved printing techniques have put good reproductions within reach of those who cannot afford to buy original paintings for their homes. Although private patronage of the arts may have declined, government and municipal patronage has increased: art collections, museums, theatres, opera houses are being subsidised from public funds on a scale undreamt of in Schiller's time. An organisation like the Arts Council brings drama, ballet, and music to remote provincial corners which cannot support their own companies. And thanks to a reduction of working hours in most industries and trades, more and more people have sufficient leisure to seize all these varied opportunities of aesthetic education.

There is little doubt, then, that the remedy which Schiller proposes is available, and available in quantity. There remains the crucial question—will it work? And how exactly is it supposed to take effect? One could wish that Schiller had been a little more explicit on this point. It is not easy to see how the aesthetic can be (to quote Carlyle's words) "a necessary means of improvement among political societies",[1] and Carlyle does not stand alone in feeling sceptical about the whole idea. One finds, indeed, that those who are most keenly interested in matters of art are generally the first to grow restive at the suggestion that art should serve any purpose outside itself, political, moral, or therapeutic. The creation and the enjoyment of art, they would say, are ends in themselves, and require no sanction of any kind. In fairness to Schiller it must be said at once that he himself entirely agrees with this. He does not envisage any direct effect of aesthetic activity on the conduct of public affairs or the standards of private morality; on the contrary, he states over and over again that art cannot be expected to exert any such direct influence. "Art", he writes,[2] "never performs any particular function in its effect on man, and one could not choose a more unsuitable instrument in order to have some specific purpose, some detail, efficiently attended to. Its sphere of action is the totality of human nature, and only in so far as it influences a man's character can it affect his individual actions". And again, in the twenty-third of the *Letters on the Aesthetic Education of Man:* "It has

[1] J. A. Froude, *Thomas Carlyle*, London, 1882, Vol. I, p. 196.
[2] *Über das Pathetische.*

been explicitly proved that beauty yields no results either in the sphere of the intellect or of the will, that it does not meddle with any matter of reflection or decision, that it merely creates the capacity for both, but does not in any way determine the actual use made of this capacity". Clearly one cannot hope to settle an international dispute by organizing an international festival of art, or to resolve a private moral dilemma by going to a symphony concert, and Schiller nowhere suggests any shortcut of this kind. What he has in mind is a long-term effect. Aesthetic culture will not teach men what to do in any specific situation; but it may, Schiller thinks, help to produce men who will, in any situation that may present itself, act charitably and generously, without selfishness, greed, or malice: men who will bring to their day-to-day affairs the serenity that characterizes aesthetic experience.

At the end of his critical reflections, Schiller thus leaves us with a Pisgah-sight of the Promised Land. To the wanderers in the wilderness this may seem cold comfort. Angry young men and cynical older men will feel inclined to brush Schiller's ideas aside as mere academic theorizing or a vague messianic hope, edifying, perhaps, but unrealistic. Even those who agree with his analysis of our modern civilisation—and it is difficult not to agree with it—may object that though his premisses are sound, his conclusion lacks the force of proof. Granted that what is needed to restore our modern world to health is a new spiritual climate, a change of heart; granted further that such a change can only be achieved through some process of progressive education, it does not necessarily follow that *aesthetic* education is the best way, or the only way, to bring it about. In fact, it may be argued that those who have actually undergone some measure of aesthetic education—artists and devotees of the arts—are not usually noted for displaying, either in their private lives or in their public utterances, that calm detachment and that generous tolerance which Schiller takes to be the mark of the aesthetic state. Is it possible, in face of these objections, to give assent to Schiller's views? The answer would seem to depend on what is meant by "assent" in a situation where logical certainty is unattainable and where the evidence of experience is, at best, inconclusive. In such a case, assent or dissent becomes a matter of choice, a deliberate throwing in of one's lot one way or the other. In a different context one might call it an act of faith, remembering that faith has been described as the substance of things hoped for.

When one is talking about Schiller one often feels tempted, and sometimes compelled, to use the language of theology. At first sight this seems strange, for Schiller was critical of the dogmas of revealed religion, and his attitude to the Church may be defined as one of benevolent neutrality. But though his simple boyhood faith did not long survive his boyhood, the religious upbringing which he had received left a permanent mark on the cast of his mind. The basic concepts of Christian belief—redemption through sacrifice, sin and atonement, a paradise lost and a paradise to be regained—all these loom large in Schiller's writings, not in their orthodox Christian sense but as forms of thought and imagery in which his mind habitually moves. There is a revealing passage in one of his letters to Goethe[1] in which he speaks of Christianity as "the expression of moral grace or of the incarnation of holiness, and in that sense the only *aesthetic* religion". His plea for the aesthetic education of man may be read as a gloss—albeit a somewhat Pelagian gloss—on that most difficult injunction "Be ye therefore perfect": an attempt to justify a humanist's faith in his fellow-men. What King Philip in *Don Carlos* says of Posa, the idealist who has given his life (however fruitlessly) in the cause

1 17 August, 1795.

of human freedom, may be said of Schiller himself:

Seine Neigung war
Die Welt mit allen kommenden Geschlechtern.

That is what Goethe means—or at least part of what he means—by the simple phrase, so moving in its simplicity, which he repeats twice in his *Epilog zu Schillers Glocke:* "Denn er war unser". Of course Goethe was speaking for Schiller's personal friends, and also for the wider circle of his readers and admirers among his German compatriots; but at the same time he was speaking for mankind at large. "Let the world", he says, "be grateful for his teaching":

Die Welt verdank ihm, was er sie gelehrt.

Schiller himself was not backward when it was a question of staking his claim to the literary heritage of other countries. In his medico-philosophical dissertation of 1780, which contains several references to Shakespeare's plays, he uses an expression which has ever since given a certain amount of amusement to English critics: he speaks of "unser Shakespeare". He uses the first person of the possessive, not ignorantly nor presumptuously, but simply as a mark of affection. At a later stage, in the poem *Shakespeares Schatten*, he pictured himself meeting the shade of Shakespeare in the underworld. One would like to think that if these two playwrights really met somewhere in the Elysian fields, Shakespeare, whom the youthful Schiller had fondly, if a little naively, called "our Shakespeare", might find it in his gentle heart to acknowledge—perhaps even to return—the compliment.